ANCIENT EGYPTIAN
CROSS STITCH

BARBARA HAMMET

David and Charles

A DAVID & CHARLES BOOK
Copyright © David & Charles Limited 2006

David & Charles is an F+W Publications Inc. company
4700 East Galbraith Road
Cincinnati, OH 45236

First published in the UK in 2006

Text and designs copyright © Barbara Hammet 2006

A catalogue record for this book is available from the British Library.

ISBN-13: 978-0-7153-2243-7 hardback
ISBN-10: 0-7153-2243-5 hardback

ISBN-13: 978-0-7153-2584-1 paperback
ISBN-10: 0-7153-2584-1 paperback

Printed in China by SNP Leefung
for David & Charles
Brunel House   Newton Abbot   Devon

Executive Editor Cheryl Brown
Editor Jennifer Proverbs
Art Editor Prudence Rogers
Designer Eleanor Stafford
Project Editor and chart preparation Lin Clements
Production Controller Ros Napper

Visit our website at www.davidandcharles.co.uk

David & Charles books are available from all good bookshops; alternatively you can contact our Orderline
on 0870 9908222 or write to us at FREEPOST EX2 110, D&C Direct, Newton Abbot, TQ12 4ZZ (no stamp
required UK only); US customers call 800-289-0963 and Canadian customers call 800-840-5220.

Contents

Introduction

Ancient Egypt... whose imagination is not fired by the sight of the golden mask of Tutankhamun, of a land where the all powerful pharaoh was divine, where astonishing monuments survive the encroaching sands of the desert, keeping their secrets intact within their massive stones?

For centuries the exciting and distinctive civilization of the Ancient Egyptians has captured our imagination with its beautiful art and architecture and intrigued us with the skill and genius they reveal. Over 5,000 years ago, under the rule of the pharaohs, the Ancient Egyptians created a complex cosmology to explain the world and a pantheon of mighty gods to control it.

The rediscovery of Ancient Egypt is a long but splendid tale of adventure and detection, beginning during Napoleon Bonaparte's military campaign in Egypt at the end of the 18th century, when pyramids, temples and statues were discovered that excited Europe and America and began a popular Egyptian, or 'Empire', fashion, and one of Bonaparte's officers recovered a portentous inscribed slab of black granite at Rosetta.

Long before this, the Greek historian Herotodus (*circa* 485–425 BC) had written of the

One of Egypt's most famous and awe-inspiring treasures is the immense sculpture of the Great Sphinx at Giza, carved from solid stone over 4,500 years ago

Egyptians, reporting some of their customs and astutely understanding the significance of the river Nile to Egyptian life. Indeed, without the great river Nile, Egypt might never have become a prosperous and powerful nation. Flowing through the length of the country, it was a vital feature in the lives of the Ancient Egyptians, both in terms of trade and the yearly flooding, which created productive tracts of land in a country hemmed in by the driest of desert sands.

The presence and rhythm of the river Nile helped to create stability and wealth, and Ancient Egypt developed into a highly organized society with a sophisticated bureaucracy. Spiritually, Egyptians paid homage and made offerings to the gods, who they expected to protect them. They often wore amulets for luck. People carried them in life and were buried with them wrapped into their mummies, to protect them in the afterlife. The most popular were those that warded off danger or promised good health, such as the Eye of Horus.

The Ancient Egyptians worshipped many fascinating gods. Horus, a falcon-headed god, represented power and kingship, while the goddess Hathor represented love, fertility and child birth

The Ancient Egyptians' most noticeable relics, the pyramids, bear witness to their primary obsession, with death and continued existence in the afterlife. The Egyptians believed that the body, and especially its name, needed to be preserved. Pyramids could keep the bodies safe through the centuries. Preserving the bodies involved embalming them and wrapping in preservative bandages to form the mummies we can still see in museums today. When first built, the pyramids had, at their peak, a gilded feature that caught the rays of the sun and provided a stepping stone to the kingdom of the Sun for the dead pharaoh entombed in the pyramid.

The Egyptians recognized a great number of gods, many of them shown with animal heads, like Anubis who was depicted as a man with a jackal's head. Their greatest sky god was Re, the Sun, represented by a red circle, and this is featured in the falcon box on page 48. Goddesses like Hathor and Isis, as well as having magical properties were seen as embodiments of motherhood and often appear as little statues, with a child on the knee. Protection, health and fertility were important qualities offered by gods, for example the goddess Isis, who magically restored her dead husband to life.

Gods were worshipped in huge temples dedicated to them and served by priests. Many of these fabulous buildings remain today, helping to make Egypt a 'must see' holiday destination – who has not longed to see the atmospheric Temple at Luxor with its obelisk reaching up to the sun, or enter the mind-blowing Great Pyramid at Giza? My designs on page 54 and 56 try to bring these treasures a step closer.

As well as having well-developed spiritual beliefs, Ancient Egypt was also a highly literate society, its written language that of the hieroglyphs. This fascinating language, as well as using captivating images, was a vital tool for recording knowledge but for centuries it stubbornly withheld its secrets, defying the cleverest code-breakers. Eventually, Jean Francois

Champollion (1790–1832) used the Rosetta Stone to begin deciphering their meaning. Years of study revealed that hieroglyphic writing was used to record law, geography, astronomy, mathematics, medicine, poetry and mythological stories. Some of the hieroglyphs feature on the desk set on page 61.

Like the hieroglyphs, Ancient Egyptian art is very distinctive: gods and humans were shown with each part of the body in its most recognisable aspect. The gods I've included in the Monument Panel on page 9 are typical – heads, arms and legs are shown in profile, shoulders from the front. The face of the Egyptian Queen on page 25 is shown from the side view but the eye is shown from the front.

Though we admire the art of the Ancient Egyptians, they considered themselves as craftsmen and were highly skilled masters of carving, metalwork and painting. Painted animals and figures are enlarged versions of hieroglyphic symbols. Much of what we know of their way of life and beliefs is gained from the ideal lifestyle painted in the tombs in hopes that the deceased would enjoy it everlastingly

Hieroglyphs look like stylized pictures but they are an ancient and complex language that continues to reveal intriguing details about the lives and beliefs of the Ancient Egyptian people

in the afterlife. The discovery of a young pharaoh's tomb in 1922 by British Egyptologist Howard Carter lead to the fabulous treasures of Tutankhamun travelling the world, bringing a sense of romance and excitement to a whole new generation and inspiring new fashions.

No ancient civilization arouses such universal passion and awe as the Egypt of the pharaohs and from this fascinating culture

Even today, Ancient Egyptian art and design continues to hold us in thrall. The falcon epitomized the god, Horus, and iconic designs such as these appear widely in tomb paintings and carved reliefs

I have selected some of the strongest images and ideas to create a unique collection of cross stitch designs. The imagery and colours used by the Ancient Egyptians are strong and evocative, making these designs striking additions to any home.

Whether you choose to make an impressive wall hanging, some elegant cushions or a beautiful bag, your work will reflect one of the most awe-inspiring and enigmatic of cultures.

These two cushions feature the two significant plants of the marshy Nile valley, the lotus and the papyrus. The lotus design here is from a pendant jewel, repeated four times

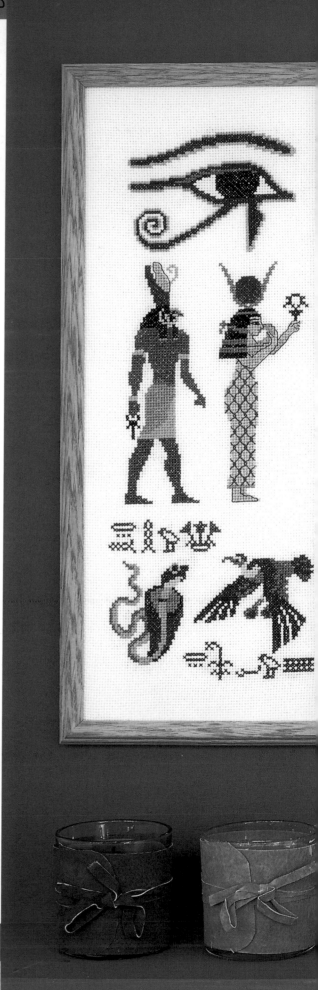

Ancient Wonders

For centuries, the smothering sands of Egypt preserved one of the most awesome monuments ever to be built – the colossal sculpture of the Great Sphinx at Giza. This creature, carved from stone with a human head and a lion's body, has long stirred the excitement and imagination of scholars, poets and

tourists. It symbolized might and power, controlled by the godlike intelligence of the Old Kingdom pharaoh, Khafre. Workers shaped this immense block of stone, giving it the face of their king, over 4,500 years ago. Between 1925 and 1936 the great beast was fully released from the sand, revealing a body 73m (240ft) long and over 20m (65ft) tall.

Like a sentinel, the sphinx guards Kafre's pyramid, which rises between the pyramids of Khufu (shown in the embroidery here) and Menkaure. My panel shows the sphinx as it is today, eroded but still magnificent as the sun sinks in the sky. The pyramids, tomb paintings and carved reliefs have revealed much about Ancient Egyptian beliefs and some of these are explored in the side panels to this piece – see pages 12 and 13.

This impressive panel is worked on a pale background to bring all the motifs into sharp relief. It uses half cross stitches rather than full stitches to add luminosity to the sky. The design is very versatile and can be used as the source for smaller projects (see pages 14 and 15).

Monument Panel

Stitch count
204 x 346
Design size
37 x 63cm (14½ x 25in)

Materials
- ☞ 56 x 82cm (22 x 32in) 14-count ivory Aida (Zweigart 264) or 28-count evenweave in a pale neutral
- ☞ Tapestry needle size 24
- ☞ Stranded cotton (floss) as listed in chart key
- ☞ Suitable picture frame

1 Prepare your fabric and mark the centre lines with tacking (basting) – see page 99. As this is a large and complex design, you may find it helpful to add further guide lines to mark the outer edges of the floral borders and the central scene.

2 Following the chart on pages 16-21 begin stitching from the centre of the chart and fabric (working over two threads if using evenweave). Use two strands of stranded cotton (floss) for the cross stitch. The sky in the central panel is worked in half cross stitch with two strands of thread throughout but you could work it in full cross stitch if you prefer.

3 Work the backstitch with one strand after the cross stitch has been completed. Wherever possible make a backstitch the length of one block of the Aida weave (though some stitches are longer, and some are only half a block).

4 When the embroidery is complete remove guide lines and press the work. Frame as a picture (see page 101 for advice).

The Monument Panel design is a large one and the chart has been divided into six parts, spread over pages 16–21, and labelled as shown here.

Part 1 (page 16)   Part 3 (page 18)   Part 5 (page 20)

Part 2 (page 17)   Part 4 (page 19)   Part 6 (page 21)

Exploring Ancient Egyptian Beliefs

The Monument Panel is filled with images that conjure up a picture of the spiritual lives of the Ancient Egyptians and some of their fascinating beliefs are described here.

On either side of the central panel, separated by pillars of flowers, are some of the important gods of Ancient Egypt. The Eyes of Horus symbolize the sun (on the left side of the panel) and the moon (the right side). The eyes had magical health-giving properties, bestowing protection and were thought to ward off bad luck.

This left-hand panel shows Horus (far left), a powerful falcon-headed god who represented power and kingship. He wears white and red crowns, which represent the union of Upper Egypt and Lower Egypt and carries the ankh sign for life.

Next to him is the goddess Hathor, with her headdress of a sun disc between cow's horns. She was a mother goddess who represented love, sexuality, fertility and child birth, and was also associated with music, dance and alcohol. The sistrum she holds up was a percussion instrument used in ceremonies. Her heavy bead necklace projected her power. She wears a long black wig and tight linen dress with an over-dress made of a network of beads.

Below Horus and Hathor, the goddess Wadjet, shown as a cobra, represented Lower Egypt. The hieroglyphs above have the same meaning. The goddess Nekhbet, shown as a vulture, represented Upper Egypt and again the hieroglyphs repeat the message. The cobra and vulture appear together as the *uraeus* on the headdress of the pharaoh.

👁 This right-hand panel shows the gods responsible for the afterlife. At the top is the Eye of Horus, which was painted on coffins and on the bows of boats, both to protect the craft and 'see' the way.

👁 Below this is the god Osiris (far right), dressed as a mummy. He was the Lord of the Afterlife and judge of the dead. His skin is green because he was also a god of agriculture and fertility and was responsible for rebirth to eternity.

👁 Standing beside Osiris is Thoth, the ibis-headed god who was scribe to the gods.

👁 Below Thoth is the jackal-headed god, Anubis, who was responsible for embalming and for cemeteries. He accompanied the dead to the throne of Osiris for the weighing of the heart ceremony (see page 72).

👁 The flower borders on either side of the central scene were inspired by those seen on the gold throne of Tutankhamun. Papyrus, which was often worn as an amulet, existed as a hieroglyph, symbolizing joy and youth. A group of three flowers symbolized the Kingdom of Lower Egypt. The lotus flower sinks below the surface of the water at night and opens as the sun rises again, symbolizing rebirth.

Eye of Horus Case

Stitch count
45 x 61
Design size
8.2 x 11cm (3¼ x 4⅛in)

Materials

- 28 x 23cm (11 x 9in) 14-count dark green Aida (DMC 500)
- Tapestry needle size 24
- Stranded cotton (floss) as listed in chart key
- Rayon floss thread, in white
- Anchor Ophir metallic thread, in gold (or other gold thread)
- Kreinik blending filament black 005HL
- Lining fabric 25 x 25cm (10 x 10in)
- Decorative cord 1m (40in)

1 Fold the fabric in half lengthways (the other half becomes the back of the case). Use the chart below, counting three blocks from the fold before beginning to embroider. Use one strand of metallic gold thread, two strands of white rayon thread and one strand of black blending filament with the black cotton.

2 Fold the fabric in half lengthways, embroidery inside. Pin the sides together above the eyebrow and the spiral end of the eye. Allow three blocks above and below the eye and about 3cm (1¼in) to the left. Machine stitch, trim off excess fabric, turn the case to the right side and press from the back. At the open end fold the fabric in 2cm (¾in) from the design and press. Unfold again and trim the folded area to 4cm (1½in).

3 Fold the lining fabric in half and make a replica bag. Press with the seam on the outside. Fold the open end over so that the lining will be 2.5cm (1in) shorter than the finished case will be. The folded-over lining should face the same side as the seam, so the inside is smooth. Press the fold and trim off the excess, leaving 1.25cm (½in) turning allowance. Assemble the case with the lining inside and then slipstitch the folded turning of the lining to the inside of the case.

4 Decorate with a cord, slipstitching it to the sides of the case and allowing enough for a strap at the top and sufficient for fraying out two tassels at the bottom.

The Eye of Horus motif was the inspiration for this striking glasses case.

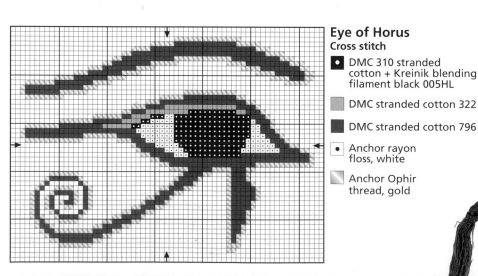

Eye of Horus
Cross stitch

- ● DMC 310 stranded cotton + Kreinik blending filament black 005HL
- DMC stranded cotton 322
- DMC stranded cotton 796
- · Anchor rayon floss, white
- Anchor Ophir thread, gold

Papyrus Card

Stitch count
32 x 31
Design size
6 x 6cm (2¼ x 2¼in)

Materials

- 15 x 15cm (6 x 6in) 14-count Rustico Aida
- Tapestry needle size 24
- Stranded cotton (floss) as listed in chart key (you will only need a few of the colours)
- 15 x 15cm (6 x 6in) fusible interfacing
- Greetings card with 8 x 8cm (3 x 3in) aperture
- Double-sided adhesive tape

1 Prepare your fabric and mark the centre lines with tacking (basting) – see page 99.

2 Following the chart on page 16, begin stitching the motif from the centre of the fabric, using two strands of stranded cotton (floss) for cross stitch.

3 When the embroidery is complete remove guides and press. Iron fusible interfacing on the back and mount the embroidery in your card (see page 101).

You could work the Monument Panel as two separate pictures – one consisting of the central scene and flower borders and the other made up of the left-hand section arranged next to the right-hand section.

For a really contemporary look, work the left, centre and right parts of the design as three individual pictures, then frame them similarly and hang together as an impressive split panel.

Select any of the flowers from the borders for small projects such as cards or coasters or to stitch an embroidered patch, perhaps with frayed edges, to attach to a book cover. Change the colours as you please. Try using bands of three or more flowers for colourful bookmarks or to frame pictures or mirrors, or arrange the flowers side by side, perhaps divided by zigzag bands.

You could work other small scenes from the main panel, such as this picture of the gods Horus and Hathor. It was stitched on 28-cream Vintage Cashel linen to create an authentic aged look.

➘	310
	316
	322 (2 skeins)
⊤	340
−	402
⌐	436
╲	437
	561
	562
	721
⊥	738
✕	741
○	754
●	782
	796 (2 skeins)
✚	817
	844
	938
▷	972 (4 skeins)
	977
−	3325
⊙	3726
╱	3740 (2 skeins)
	3835
	3849
	3855 (2 skeins)
	3856 (2 skeins)
	3862 (3 skeins)
•	B5200

Backstitch

—	310
—	938
—	972
—	3726
—	3849
—	3855

You will need 1 skein, or less, of each colour but 2 skeins of 322, 796, 3740, 3855 and 3856, 3 skeins of 3862 and 4 skeins of 972

Part 1

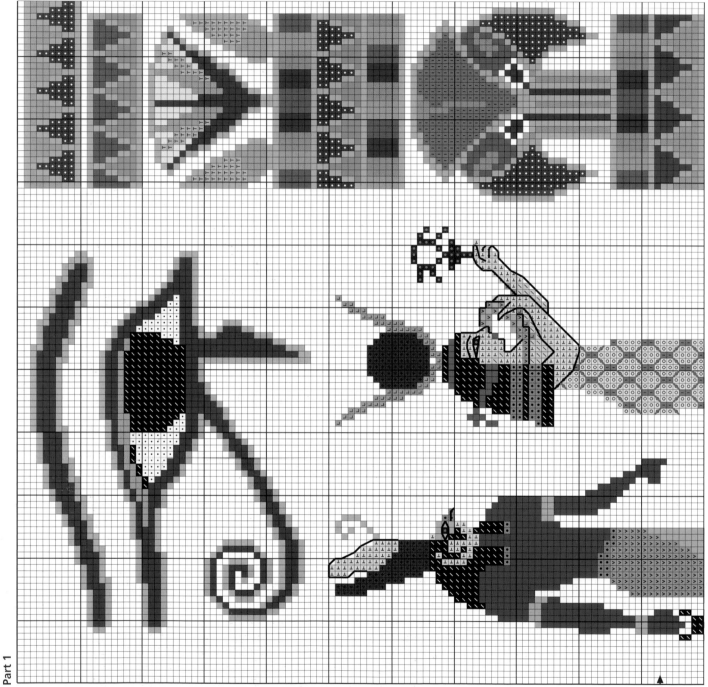

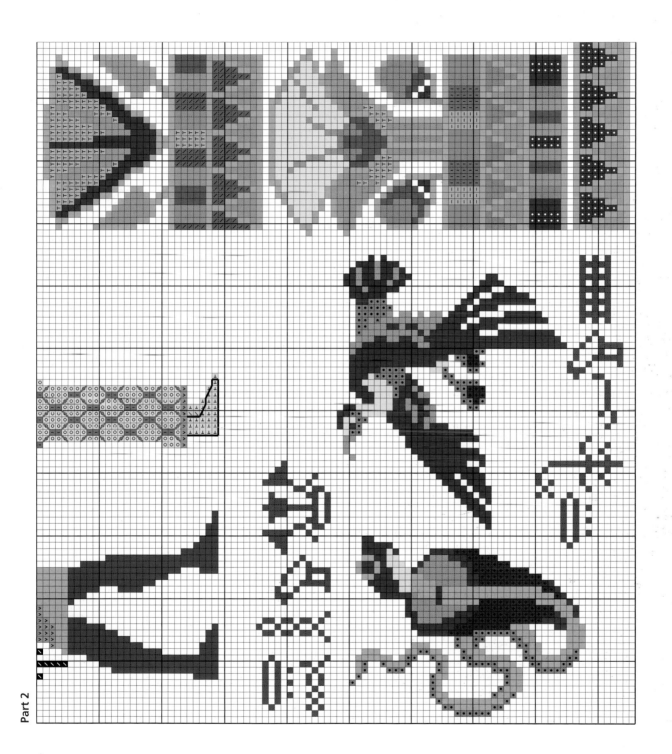

Monument Panel
DMC stranded cotton
Cross stitch

310	316	322 (2 skeins)	340	402	436	437	561	562	721	738	741	754	782	796 (2 skeins)	817	844	938	972 (4 skeins)	977	3325	3726	3740 (2 skeins)	3835	3849	3855 (2 skeins)	3856 (2 skeins)	3862 (3 skeins)	B5200

Part 4

Backstitch

——	310
||	938
| |	972
| |	3726
| |	3849
| |	3855

Sky area: stitch colours within outline in half cross stitch with 2 strands

You will need 1 skein, or less, of each colour but 2 skeins of 322, 796, 3740, 3855 and 3856, 3 skeins of 3862 and 4 skeins of 972

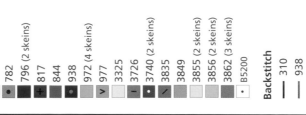

✎	310
	316
	322 (2 skeins)
T	340
	402
	436
L	437
	561
	562
	721
⊥	738
X	741
○	754
●	782
	796 (2 skeins)
+	817
	844
●	938
∨	972 (4 skeins)
	977
−	3325
●	3726
╱	3740 (2 skeins)
	3835
	3849
	3855 (2 skeins)
	3856 (2 skeins)
	3862 (3 skeins)
·	B5200

Backstitch

——	310
——	938
——	972
——	3726
——	3849
——	3855

You will need 1 skein, or
less, of each colour but 2
skeins of 322, 796, 3740,
3855 and 3856, 3 skeins of
3862 and 4 skeins of 972

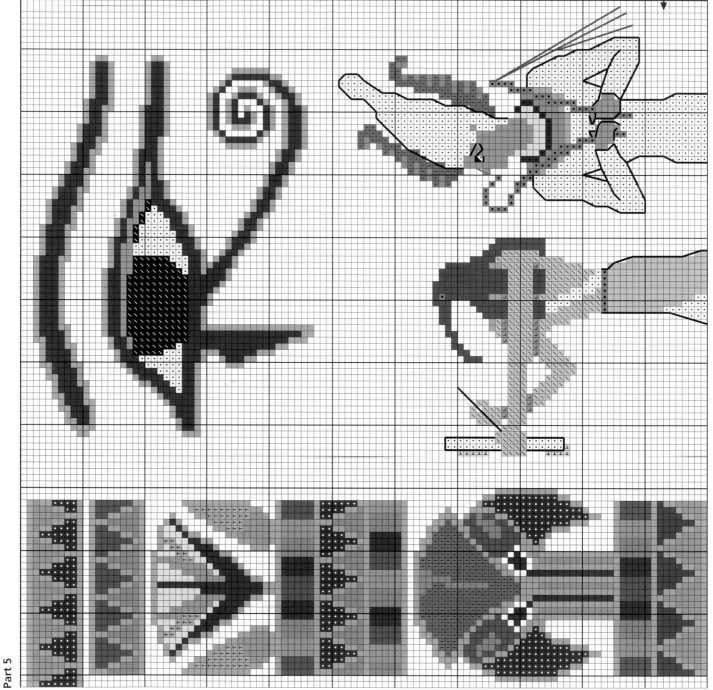

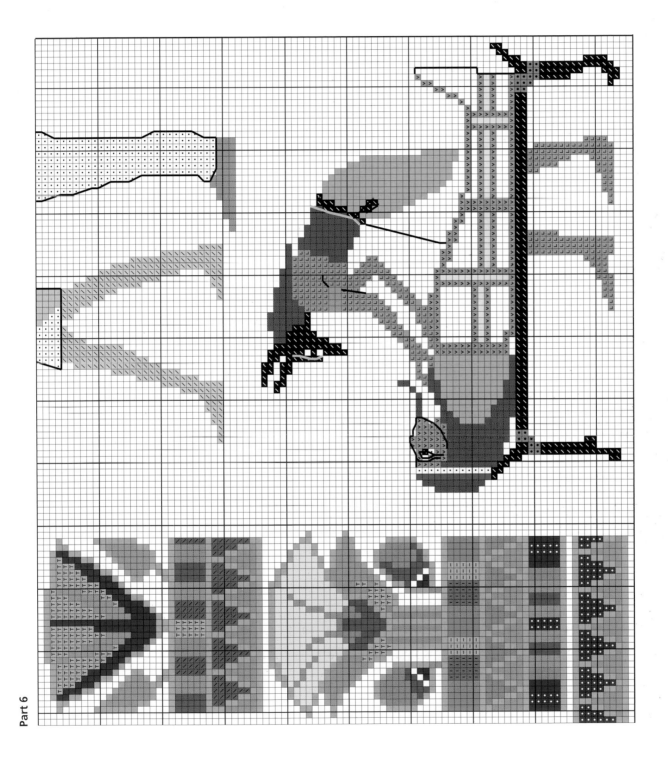

Gods on Earth

Pharaoh... across thousands of years the word still conjures up all that is memorable and magnificent from Ancient Egypt; absolute rulers who brought order, education and invention and celebrated their reigns with magnificent monuments, many of which still draw travellers to Egypt today.

To the Ancient Egyptians their pharaoh became a living god at his coronation, who spoke for his people to the many immortal gods they worshipped. He was described as Son of Re, the almighty Sun god, and as Horus, the falcon god. The pharaoh's wives and children were also regarded by the Egyptians as divine.

The pharaoh most widely recognised today is the 'boy king' Tutankhamun who reigned in the New Kingdom period, from 1332–1322BC. The discovery of his tomb in the Valley of the Kings by the British Egyptologist Howard Carter in 1922 created a huge sensation. The tomb was filled to overflowing with all kinds of fabulous golden treasures, the innermost coffin of solid gold holding the masked mummy of the King.

The mask of Tutankhamun, on which my design opposite is based, is a stunning image of power and majesty. At the same time, the modelling of the features reminds us that the mummy is of a youth barely 19 when he died. He wears a wig inlaid with blue glass and a curved plaited beard which is a symbol of divinity. His eyes are inlaid with quartz and obsidian. On his brow he wears the *uraeus*, a female cobra that is a symbol of Lower Egypt and a vulture, representing the goddess Nekhbet, protector of Upper Egypt.

This Tutankhamun design has a companion, shown on page 25. My inspiration for the queen came from a limestone relief carving from the same New Kingdom period (this queen was actually the consort of pharaoh Amenophis III). She wears a crown of cobras surmounted by sun discs, representing the sun god and kingship. On her wig a band bears the falcon Horus, his protective wings encircling her head. I have added a gold collar with a garland of petals, as shown in paintings of the time. She carries a blue lotus flower, another symbol of the sun and creation.

This impressive Tutankhamun design uses cross stitch and is straightforward to stitch. The gleaming, golden look is created just by subtle shading of the embroidery cottons. On his chest the collar is inlaid with imitation coloured beads and petals. The border pattern is derived from decoration found in Tutankhamun's tomb, and this is repeated in the Egyptian Queen design on page 25.

Stitch count (for each design)
211 x 139
Design size
38.3 x 25.2cm (15 x 10in)

Materials (for each design)
- 46 x 35cm (18 x 14in) 14-count antique white Aida (DMC 712)
- Tapestry needle size 24
- Stranded cotton (floss) as listed in chart key
- Iron-on interfacing 46 x 35cm (18 x 14in) (optional)
- Suitable picture frame

Many pharaoh's crowns featured the uraeus, a rearing female cobra that indicated the pharaoh was protector of his realm. A tightly plaited false beard was also worn by the pharaoh: such beards were seen as an attribute of the gods only, so were further evidence of the pharaoh's divine status.

1 Prepare your fabric and mark the centre lines with tacking (basting) – see page 99. It would be helpful to add extra guide lines in another colour, 30 blocks above and below, to right and to left to help keep your place. Both of these designs are intensively stitched pieces that are worth mounting on an embroidery frame to help prevent distortion.

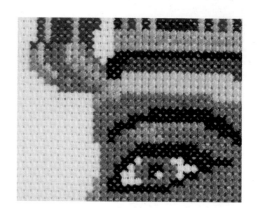

2 Following the relevant chart (Tutankhamun on pages 26–27 and the Egyptian Queen on page 28–29), begin stitching from the centre of the chart and fabric, using two strands of stranded cotton (floss) for the cross stitch. Also use two strands of cotton (floss) for the backstitch, which only appears in Tutankhamun's beard (see right). With long slanting backstitch lines, take a fresh stitch where the line crosses an intersection on the chart. It is worthwhile at an early stage to count out to the decorative border and begin to stitch the yellow inner edge of the strong, simple pattern.

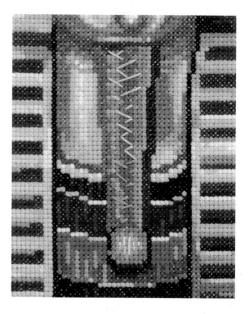

3 When the embroidery is complete remove the guide lines and press the work. Frame as a picture (see page 101 for advice).

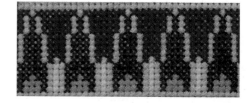

A pharaoh could have many wives; most of them had little power but there was usually a single 'Great Wife' and this queen was regarded as the pharaoh's official consort. In many cases she was a close blood relative. This beautiful and beguiling design is a profile view, very typical of Ancient Egyptian art, which represented things in their most typical and recognisable aspect. It can be stitched as a companion to the Tutankhamun design on the previous page and above. They could both be worked as framed pictures or would make two stunning wall hangings or fire screens.

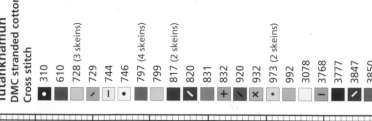

Tutankhamun

DMC stranded cotton

Cross stitch

Symbol	Colour
▣	310
■	610
□	728 (3 skeins)
╱	729
❘	744
•	746
■	797 (4 skeins)
■	799
╱	817 (2 skeins)
■	820
+	831
╲	832
✕	920
•	932
■	973 (2 skeins)
□	992
▬	3078
▬	3768
■	3777
╱	3847
■	3850

Backstitch (use 2 strands)

— 729

— 973

— 3078

You will need 1 skein, or less, of each colour but 4 skeins of 797, 3 skeins of 728 and 2 skeins each of 817 and 973

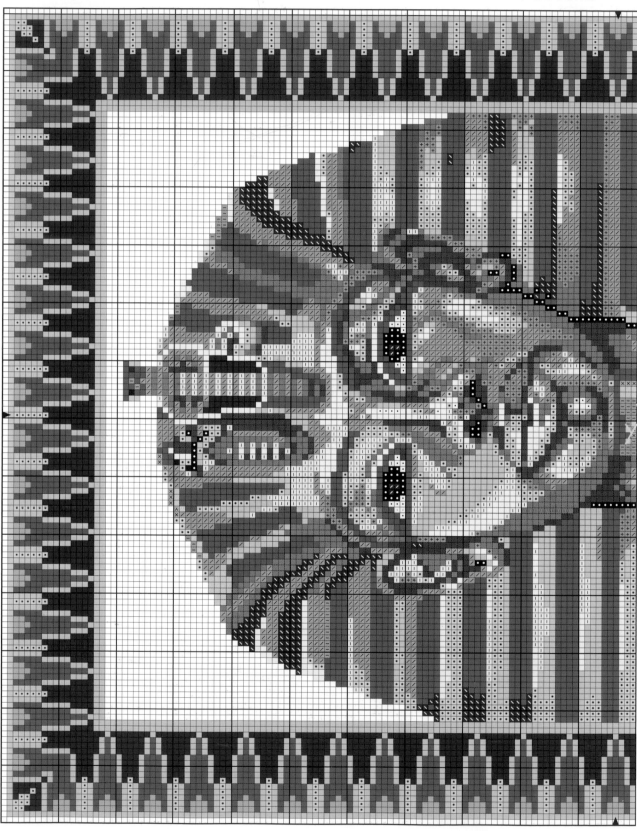

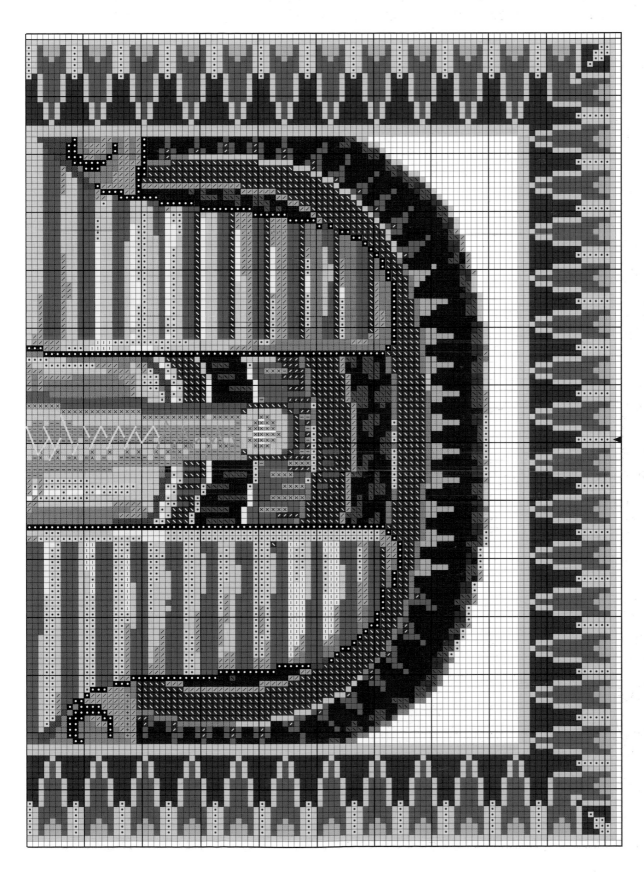

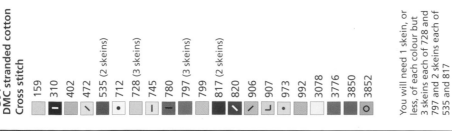

Egyptian Queen
DMC stranded cotton
Cross stitch

159	
310	▬
402	
472	╲
535 (2 skeins)	
712	•
728 (3 skeins)	
745	I
780	▬
797 (3 skeins)	
799	
817 (2 skeins)	
820	╲
906	╱
907	∟
973	•
992	
3078	
3776	
3850	
3852	O

You will need 1 skein, or less, of each colour but 3 skeins each of 728 and 797 and 2 skeins each of 535 and 817

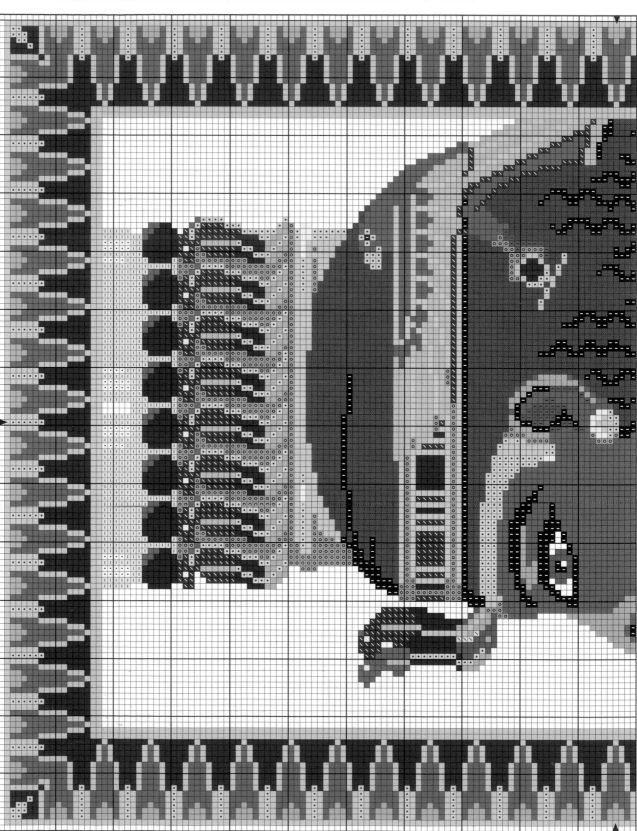

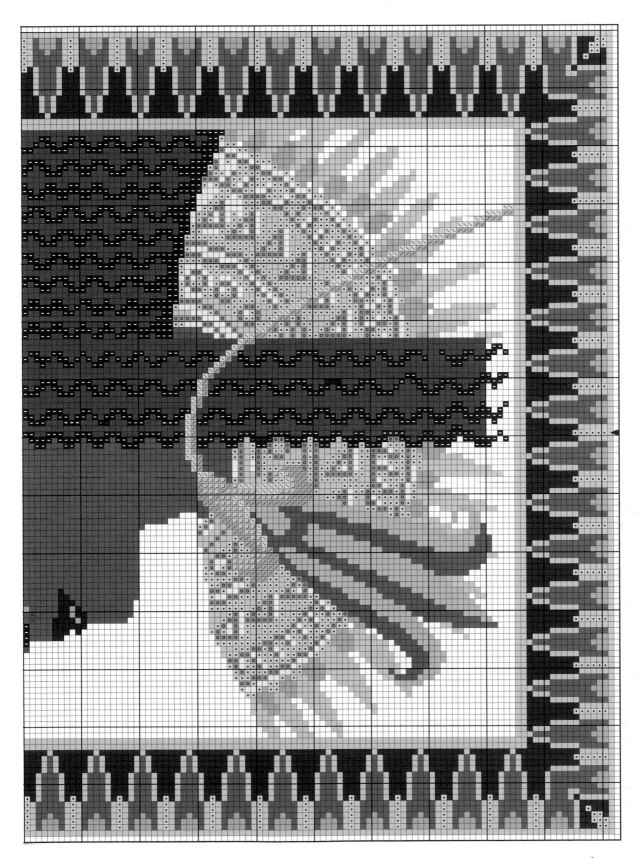

The Royal Hunt

Full speed across the desert in a horse-drawn chariot – this exciting scene was inspired by a painting on a casket found in the tomb of Tutankhamun. Every surface of the casket is covered in detailed decoration. The pharaoh is shown driving his chariot, pulled by lively and richly plumed and tasselled horses. He is hunting in the desert with his bow and arrow, accompanied by his hounds as they chase wild asses, antelope, striped hyena and ostriches. In the original piece there is a greater crowd of animals being hunted than it was possible to show in this cross stitch version. I omitted the hieroglyphic messages, the fan bearers and hunt followers as well, but the sparse vegetation is copied from the original. The sides of the casket have scenes showing the pharaoh pursuing Nubians and other enemies of Egypt.

Recent research shows that Tutankhamun died young, possibly as a result of an injury from a fall, but through stitching this scene his pleasure in the speed and the excitement of the chase lives on.

This exciting hunting scene is worked on a Vintage fabric that has an uneven 'antique' colouring, to suggest the desert's uneven surface. A regular geometric border is enclosed with backstitch, with repeated flowers creating a final border. This embroidery relies on a palette of subtle natural colours so it is important to work in a good light.

Royal Hunt Wall Hanging

Stitch count
199 x 379
Design size
36.3 x 69cm (14¼ x 27in)

Materials

- 55 x 85cm (21½ x 33½in)
  14-count beige Vintage Aida
  or 28-count Cashel linen
  (Zweigart 3009), or other
  neutral evenweave
- Tapestry needle size 24
- Stranded cotton (floss) as
  listed in chart key
- Fusible heavy Vilene
  0.5m (½yd)
- Decorative braid to trim
  1m (1yd)
- Blue rayon floss for tassels
- Thin wooden dowel 1m (1yd)
  for hanging
- Leather thong 1m (1yd) to
  suspend the hanging

1 Prepare your fabric and mark the centre lines with tacking (basting) – see page 99. As this is a large design, it would help to add extra guide lines, in another colour, to mark the inner border position.

Part 1 (page 34) Part 3 (page 36) Part 5 (page 38)

Part 2 (page 35) Part 4 (page 37) Part 6 (page 39)

The Royal Hunt design is a large one and the chart has been divided into six parts, spread over pages 34–39, split and labelled as shown here.

2 Following the chart on pages 34–39, begin stitching from the centre of the chart and fabric (working over two threads if using linen). You could photocopy the chart for your own use and tape the parts together. Use two strands of stranded cotton (floss) for cross stitch and one for backstitch. Wherever possible make a backstitch the length of one Aida block or two threads of linen. However, some of the diagonal backstitched lines, such as the bow string and arrows, take the cotton some distance. Judge the position by the placing of the cross stitch.

3 When all the embroidery is complete remove guide lines, press and make up as a hanging, as follows. Trim the embroidery to within about 4cm (1½in) of the stitching on either side, and about 7.6cm (3in) at the top and bottom. Cut a piece of Vilene and fuse it to the back of the embroidered fabric. Turn and hem the left and right edges neatly and then the bottom edge. Turn the top edge over to the back of the embroidery by 1.25cm (½in) and then by a further 5cm (2in) to create a channel for the dowelling and stitch in place.

4 Arrange your braid along the bottom edge, turn the ends to the back of the hanging and stitch or glue the braid to the fabric. Insert the length of wooden dowel into the channel. You can embellish your hanging by making tassels to decorate the ends of the dowel. Wind rayon floss round a 14cm (5½in) piece of card, slip it off and wind a length of the same colour round tightly near the top. Tie a knot and thread the ends through the knot to join the tassel ends and then trim.

The Royal Hunt
DMC stranded cotton
Cross stitch

Stitch count: 199 x 379

You will need 1 skein, or less, of each colour but
2 skeins each of 780 and 975 and 5 skeins of 311

Backstitch

— 310
— 435
— 918
— 930

The Royal Hunt 𓂀 35

Stitch count: 199 x 379

You will need 1 skein, or less, of each colour but
2 skeins each of 780 and 975 and 5 skeins of 311

The Royal Hunt
DMC stranded cotton
Cross stitch

∟	167		350
◨	310		352
◙	311 (5 skeins)	I	435

╱	677	◼	780 (2 skeins)	▨	918
V	720	■	782	+	922
•	746	■	898	■	930

O	972	•	977
◉	975 (2 skeins)	╱	3371
■	976	▨	3827

| ▨ | 3855 |
| I | 3856 |

Backstitch
──	310
──	435
──	918
──	930

Part 6

The Royal Hunt
DMC stranded cotton
Cross stitch

Stitch count: 199 x 379

You will need 1 skein, or less, of each colour but
2 skeins each of 780 and 975 and 5 skeins of 311

Backstitch

L	167
■	310
◉	311 (5 skeins)

■	350
▨	352
I	435

╱	677
V	720
•	746

▨	780 (2 skeins)
+	782
■	898

▨	918
+	922
■	930

O	972
•	977
╱	975 (2 skeins)
▨	976

	3855
—	3856

●	977
╱	3371
	3827

Backstitch

▬	310
▬	435
▬	918
▬	930

Isis, Winged Goddess

This elegant picture celebrates Isis, a beautiful and magical goddess who was the principle goddess of Egypt for almost 3,500 years and the personification of the faithful wife and devoted mother. She was the sister and wife of Osiris, lord of the Underworld and judge of the dead. A mistress of magic, she was fiendishly clever and was able to transform herself into different forms, notably birds, so she is often seen with kite's wings, as shown here. She was a great healer and protector, healing her son Horus when he was poisoned by a scorpion.

This cross stitch design shows Isis as she appears on painted sarcophagi cases, where she is present as a protector of the dead. The dress she wears in the embroidery is like the one she is usually seen in, which has a network of beads (some pieces of similar beadwork survive) worn over a simple linen lining. It was obviously desirable to recreate her gown out of beads, to give her a magical sparkle.

Isis, transformed into an astonishing bird, looks magnificent in a crystal-beaded gown. The pattern on the dress is formed by bugle beads while frosted seed beads complete the pattern on the wings. Some fractional stitches are used for the facial features and backstitch enhances the eye.

Isis Picture

Stitch count
94 x 281
Design size
17 x 51cm (6¾ x 20in)

Materials

- 30 x 64cm (12 x 25in) 28-count evenweave in smoky violet (Zweigart Juliana 5012)
- Tapestry needle size 24 and a beading needle
- Stranded cotton (floss) as listed in chart key
- Seed beads and bugle beads as listed in chart key
- Suitable picture frame

Isis was associated with motherly devotion and was frequently sculpted with a child on her lap, an image that is sometimes seen as a precursor to the iconic Virgin and Child pose.

1 Prepare your fabric and mark the centre lines with tacking (basting) – see page 99. It would be helpful to add extra guide lines, in another colour, 60 stitches to the left and to the right. You may find it helpful to use an embroidery frame.

2 Following the chart overleaf, begin stitching from the centre of the chart and fabric, working over two threads of evenweave. Use two strands of stranded cotton (floss) for the cross stitch and then one strand for backstitch. Wherever possible make a backstitch the length of one block of the Aida weave or two threads of linen. The face requires some three-quarter cross stitches and some fractional backstitches (see detail below).

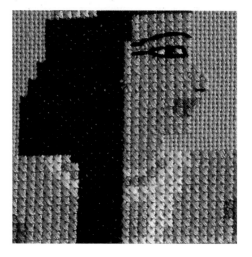

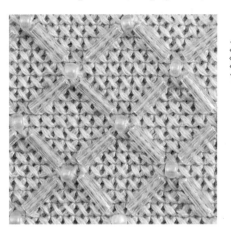

3 Stitch on the beads using a single strand of thread in the underlying colour in the positions shown on the chart. If the embroidery needs a stern pressing do this before adding the beads. Note, that some of the same bead colours are used again in the Scarab Bag on page 74, so leftover beads can be used for that project.

4 When all stitching is complete remove guide lines and give the piece a final light press face down on a thick layer of towel. Make up as a framed picture (see page 101).

Osiris was a great ruler who brought peace and civilization to Egypt but was killed by his jealous brother, Seth. Osiris's wife, Isis, discovered his body but whilst fetching her son, Seth stole the body and cut it into pieces, which he scattered far and wide. Isis and her sister Nephthys searched for and found these pieces and then changed into kites, beating their wings and fanning the air to return breath and life to Osiris.

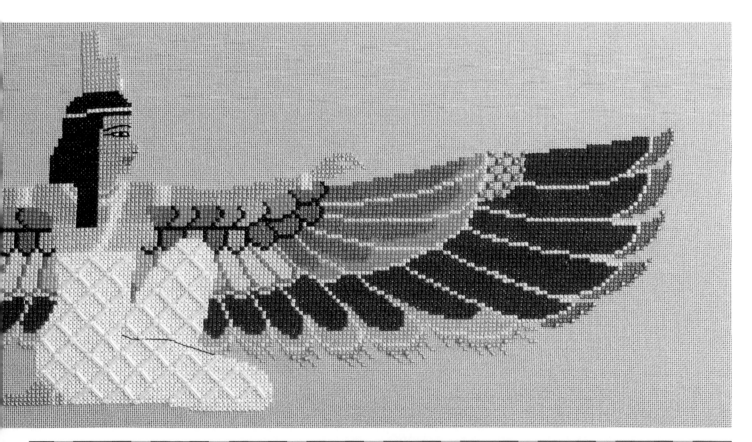

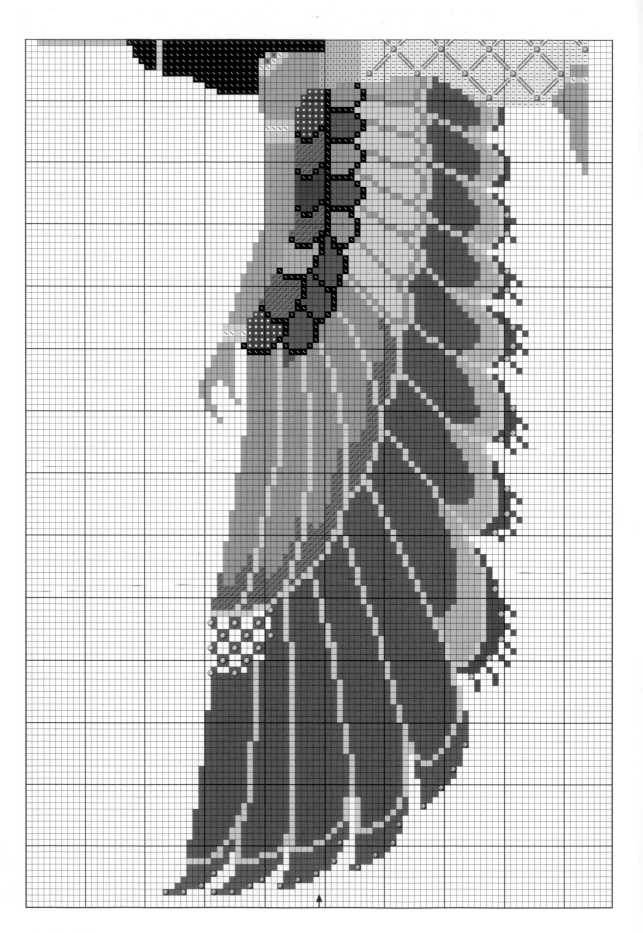

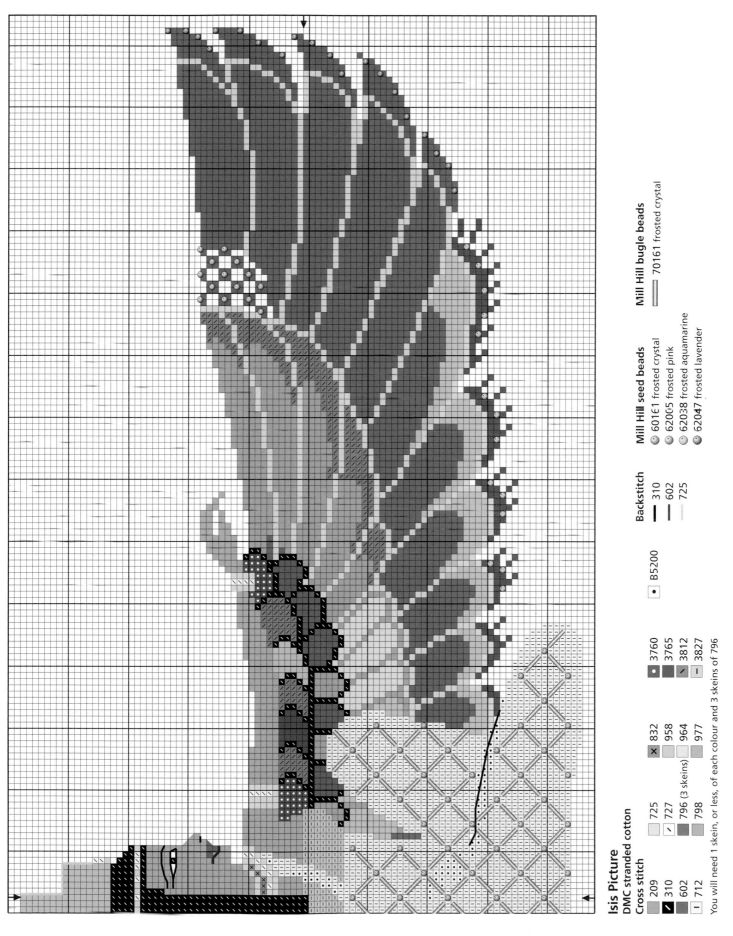

Isis Picture
DMC stranded cotton
Cross stitch

▨ 209	▨ 725	⊠ 832	◉ 3760
◪ 310	⁄ 727	⁄ 958	▨ 3765
⁄ 602	▨ 796 (3 skeins)	▨ 964	⁄ 3812
⌐ 712	⁄ 798	⌐ 977	⌐ 3827

You will need 1 skein, or less, of each colour and 3 skeins of 796

Backstitch

— 310
— 602
— 725

• B5200

Mill Hill seed beads

◉ 60161 frosted crystal
◉ 62005 frosted pink
◉ 62038 frosted aquamarine
◉ 62047 frosted lavender

Mill Hill bugle beads

▭ 70161 frosted crystal

The Regal Falcon

In Ancient Egypt the falcon was regarded as regal because it epitomized the god Horus, a great Sky God whose right eye represented the sun and his left the moon. Gods were linked with various animals and birds who shared their characteristics, so the pharaoh was often shown as a sphinx, with the body and strength of a lion. Horus was linked with the falcon because it could fly to great heights (useful for a sky god) and was swift and fierce. Horus is often shown as a falcon with his wings outspread, protecting the pharaoh. There is another Horus design on page 12, showing the god as a human.

The falcon in this embroidery was inspired by a chest ornament called a pectoral, found in the tomb of Tutankhamun. The pectoral shows the falcon as Re Harakhty (a fusion of the sun god Re and Horus), hence the sun disc on his head. The pectoral was made from gold, symbolizing the sun, and inlaid with blood-red cornelian, in

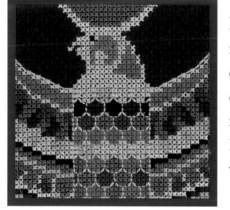

a style called cloisonné, which means the designs were outlined with strips of metal placed on the background and soldered on. The resulting cells, shaped like feathers and other features, were then filled with bright blue glass and semi-precious turquoise and cornelian.

The falcon's talons grasp hieroglyphic symbols – the ankh meaning life and the never-ending circle of the shen, which means eternity. This powerful falcon image must have impressed the Romans because the Roman eagle was clearly influenced by it.

The pectoral that inspired my embroidery is only 13cm (5in) across, smaller than this cross stitch design, but it is very beautiful, with jewel-like, precise details that I have tried to convey with clear, fresh colours. The outstretched wings and legs make it a perfect subject for a square design, which could be used to make a vivid picture, perhaps for a child's room, as well as a stunning design for a box lid.

This design uses bright colours to represent the bright glass and semi-precious materials of the original ornament. The yellow backstitch is important because it defines the feather pattern on the breast and wings. You could work this in a metallic thread if you prefer, for a gleaming gold look.

Falcon Box

Stitch count
107 x 109
Design size
19.5 x 19.8cm (7⅝ x 7¾in)

Materials

- 30 x 30cm (12 x 12in) 14-count navy Aida (Zweigart 589)
- Tapestry needle size 24
- Stranded cotton (floss) as listed in chart key
- Wooden box with 20cm (8in) square pad in lid for embroidery (see Suppliers)

1 Prepare your fabric and mark the centre lines with tacking (basting) – see page 99.

2 Following the chart opposite, begin stitching from the centre of the chart and fabric, using two strands of stranded cotton (floss) for the cross stitch and then one strand for backstitch. Wherever possible make a backstitch the length of one Aida block, though in places some backstitches will need to be longer.

3 When the embroidery is complete remove the guide lines and press the work. To mount embroidery in the box top you could leave the guide lines in the fabric temporarily to help position the embroidery over the pad. Stretch over the pad as you would over card for a picture, using linen thread (see page 101). Remove the guide lines.

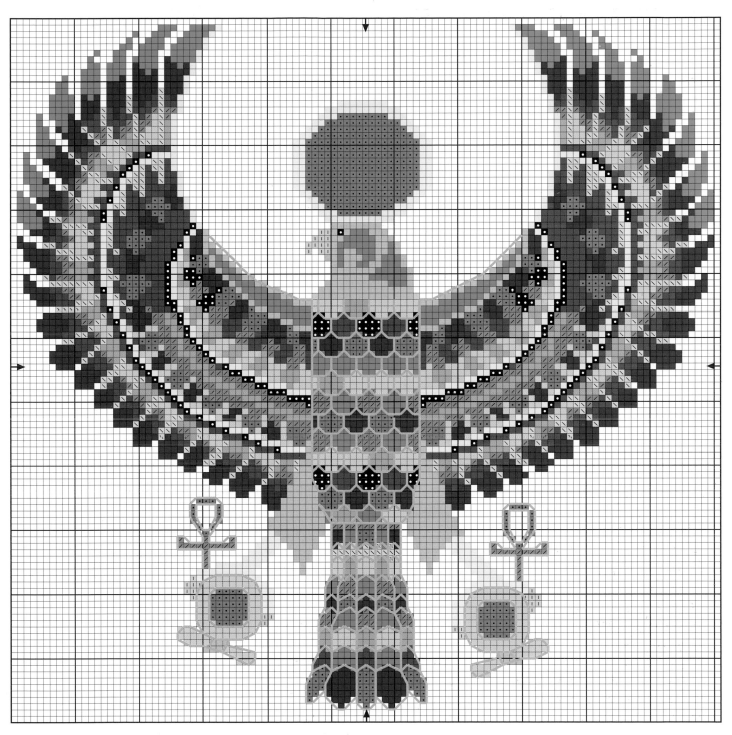

Falcon Box
DMC stranded cotton
Cross stitch

■ 666	▨ 834	▨ 972
☐ 725	• 900	▨ 995
▨ 796	◉ 939	☐ 3766
╱ 798	▨ 958	╲ 3813

You will need 1 skein, or less, of each colour

Backstitch
— 972

Magnificent Monuments

Egypt has many reminders of its glorious past civilization in the form of hundreds of temples, pyramids and statues. This chapter features designs celebrating three of the most recognizable monuments to visitors today. Two famous scenes (shown opposite) capture some of the timeless atmosphere of Ancient Egypt.

The temple at Luxor is approached through an impressive avenue of sphinxes, lions with human heads. The gateway is composed of two massive blocks of masonry that taper inwards at either end (pylon shaped) and which are incised with scenes glorifying the pharaohs. Entry is between massive seated statues of Ramesses II. The central focus of my embroidery is an obelisk, once one of a pair, the other now in the Place de la Concorde, in Paris. Obelisks originally had gilded tips to accentuate the day's first rays of sunlight.

The pyramids at Giza are a must for any tourist hoping to capture the magnificence and ambience of Ancient Egypt. In my cross stitch design I have

depicted the pyramids of Menkaure, Khafre and Khufu and they are shown silhouetted against a brilliant blue sky, beyond a vast stretch of sand, given a familiar touch by a brightly saddled camel in the foreground. The Great Pyramid of King Khufu (*circa* 2585–2560BC) is the most massive and impressive of all the pyramids.

The other design in this section (shown overleaf) is a colossal statue of Ramesses II, who was a New Kingdom pharaoh, *circa* 1279–1213BC, known also as Ramesses the Great. In his unusually long life he built and restored temples, erected statues of himself and his favourite wife, Neferati, and fought important battles against the Hittites and Syrians, which he immortalized in prose and poetry. His statue at the Karnak Temple in Luxor, the inspiration for my wall hanging, is truly enormous. In his hands he carries the flail and crook, symbols of royal power and wears the dual crown of Lower and Upper Egypt. In the embroidery his name is remembered in the cartouche, to the left.

Warm tones of old stone bring the ageless atmosphere of the temple at Luxor to this cross stitch design. The obelisk is accented by the use of long backstitches. The fabulous pyramid scene at Giza (below) is worked in whole cross stitch, with subtle colour changes for the monuments and the desert. The camel has been embellished with little tassels.

Ramesses Wall Hanging

Stitch count
130 x 90
Design size
23.5 x 16.3cm (9¼ x 6½in)

Materials

- 🔽 36 x 30cm (14 x 12in) of 14-count sky blue Aida (Zweigart 503) or 28-count evenweave
- 🔽 Tapestry needle size 24
- 🔽 Stranded cotton (floss) as listed in chart key
- 🔽 Bondaweb 36 x 30cm (14 x 12in)
- 🔽 Background fabric, a fat quarter
- 🔽 Fusible Vilene, if the background fabric needs it
- 🔽 Suede thong to trim, about 1m (1yd)
- 🔽 Four buttons
- 🔽 Thin wooden baton 35cm (14in) long
- 🔽 Fringing to trim
- 🔽 Permanent fabric glue

Statues of Ramesses II were inscribed with cartouches (oval shapes) enclosing the hieroglyphs of his official and personal names. In Ancient Egyptian times a statue was considered to be a substitute for that person, the name being more important than a superficial resemblance. And it was essential that the name be remembered or the pharaoh's spirit might be forgotten in the realm of the dead.

1 Prepare your fabric and mark the centre lines with tacking (basting) – see page 99.

2 Following the chart on page 59, begin stitching from the centre of the chart and fabric (working over two threads if using evenweave). Use two strands of stranded cotton (floss) for cross stitch and then one strand for backstitch. The backstitch is used to define the statue and hieroglyph details and it is necessary to take a number of half length backstitches and some longer ones. Take a new stitch where the line coincides with an intersection of the chart lines and, where necessary, halfway between.

3 When the embroidery is complete remove the guide lines and press the work and then make up into a wall hanging as follows. Iron Bondaweb on to the back of the embroidery and then trim the embroidery to within five Aida squares around the sides and bottom and twenty-four squares above the statue's head. Cut the background fabric to measure 50 x 37cm (20 x 14½in). Back it with fusible Vilene (if it needs stiffening) and then

turn in a 1.25cm (½in) hem along the sides and bottom, with a wider hem at the top to create a channel for the dowel. Fuse the embroidery to the centre of the background fabric and then stick a narrow edging of suede thong all round the embroidery edges, with a button at each corner to hide the joins. Sew or glue some decorative fringe to the bottom of the hanging. Feed the dowel through the top channel and use more suede thong as a hanger.

The colours used for this wall hanging are warm natural colours to evoke sun-drenched stones. The sky blue fabric makes an effective contrast. Clarity is added by the addition of backstitch. Stitching this design requires a good light as it includes subtle modelling in close shades.

Giza Scene

Stitch count
88 x 130
Design size
16 x 23.5cm (6¼ x 9¼in)

Materials

- 30 x 36cm (12 x 14in) 14-count sky blue Aida (Zweigart 503) or 28-count evenweave
- Tapestry needle size 24
- Stranded cotton (floss) as listed in chart key
- Five small tassels (optional)
- Suitable picture frame

1 Prepare your fabric and mark the centre lines with tacking (basting) – see page 99.

2 Following the chart on page 58 begin stitching from the centre of the chart and fabric (working over two threads if using evenweave). Use two strands of stranded cotton (floss) for the cross stitch and then one strand for the backstitch.

3 This design includes some little tassels – the positions are shown by little white stars on the chart. You can buy ready-made tassels or make your own, as described on the opposite page.

4 When the embroidery is complete remove the guide lines and press the work. Frame as a picture (see page 101 for advice).

The Giza pyramids are one of the wonders of the ancient world. The Great Pyramid (on the left) is Khufu's. Inside is a grand gallery leading to the burial chamber from which two shafts rise through the pyramid, aligned with significant star constellations. Khafre's pyramid, in the centre, has before it the Great Sphinx, a physical representation of Khafre. Menkaure's pyramid, the most recent, is on the right.

Making Little Tassels

Little tassels can be added to your embroidery to embellish it or to add an authentic touch, as on the camel's saddle here.

Choose a colour from the remaining stranded cottons and wind all six strands three or four times around the width of a ruler, starting and finishing with a cut end at the bottom. Slide the bunch of threads off the ruler and take a length of stranded cotton the same colour and thread it through the top of the tassel, leaving an end on either side.

Tie a knot, then wind the ends, one at a time, around the top of the bundle of cotton. Tie again. Trim the ends. Stitch in place on your cross stitch using one of the tying threads.

Luxor Scene

Stitch count
90 x 130
Design size
16.3 x 23.5cm (6½ x 9¼in)

Materials
- 30 x 36cm (12 x 14in) 14-count sky blue Aida (Zweigart 503) or 28-count evenweave
- Tapestry needle size 24
- Stranded cotton (floss) as listed in chart key
- Suitable picture frame

1 Prepare your fabric and mark the centre lines with tacking (basting) – see page 99.

2 Following the chart opposite, begin stitching from the centre of the chart and fabric (working over two threads if using evenweave). Use two strands of stranded cotton (floss) for the cross stitch and then one strand for the backstitch. The backstitch is used to define the edges of the obelisk, which requires some long stitches. Take a new stitch where the line coincides with an intersection of the chart lines.

3 When the embroidery is complete remove the guide lines and press the work. Frame as a picture (see page 101 for advice).

The Luxor temple is connected to the temple at Karnak, a short distance away, by an avenue of sphinxes. It was the setting for an annual festival dedicated to Amun, king of the gods, when statues of the gods were taken by land and river from Karnak to Luxor. This area used to be known as Thebes and was the religious capital of Egypt.

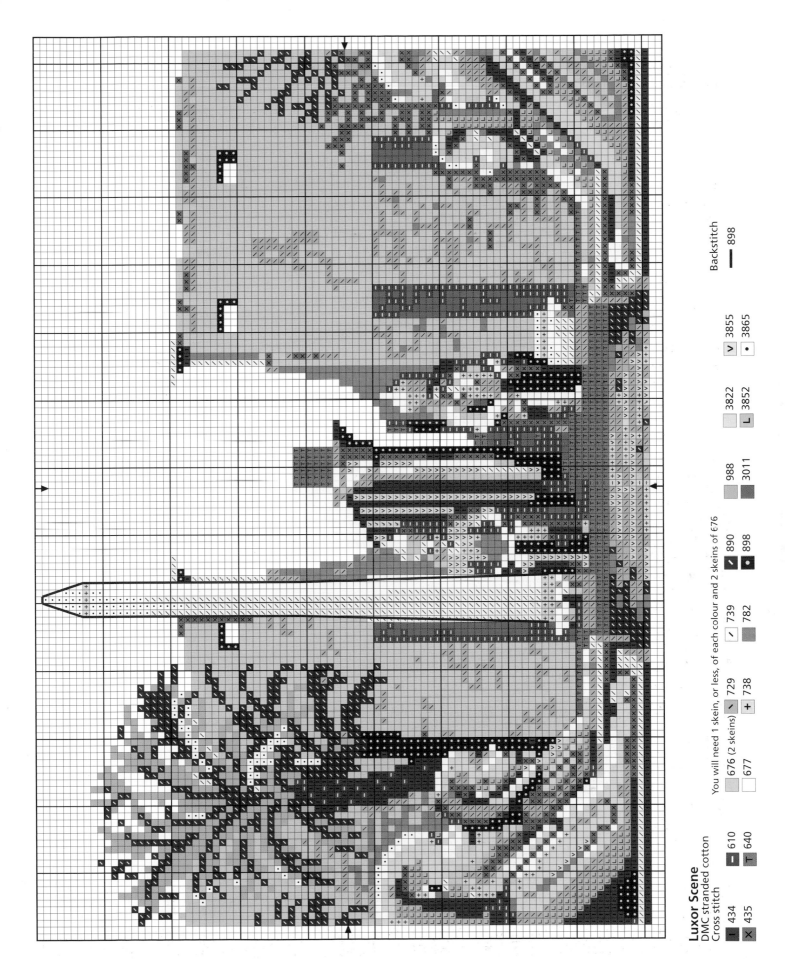

Luxor Scene
DMC stranded cotton
Cross stitch

▬	434	
X	435	

▬	610	
T	640	

You will need 1 skein, or less, of each colour and 2 skeins of 676

	676 (2 skeins)	↘	729
	677	+	738

↗	739		890
	782	◉	898

	988		3011

	3822		3852
		L	

V	3855
•	3865

Backstitch
— 898

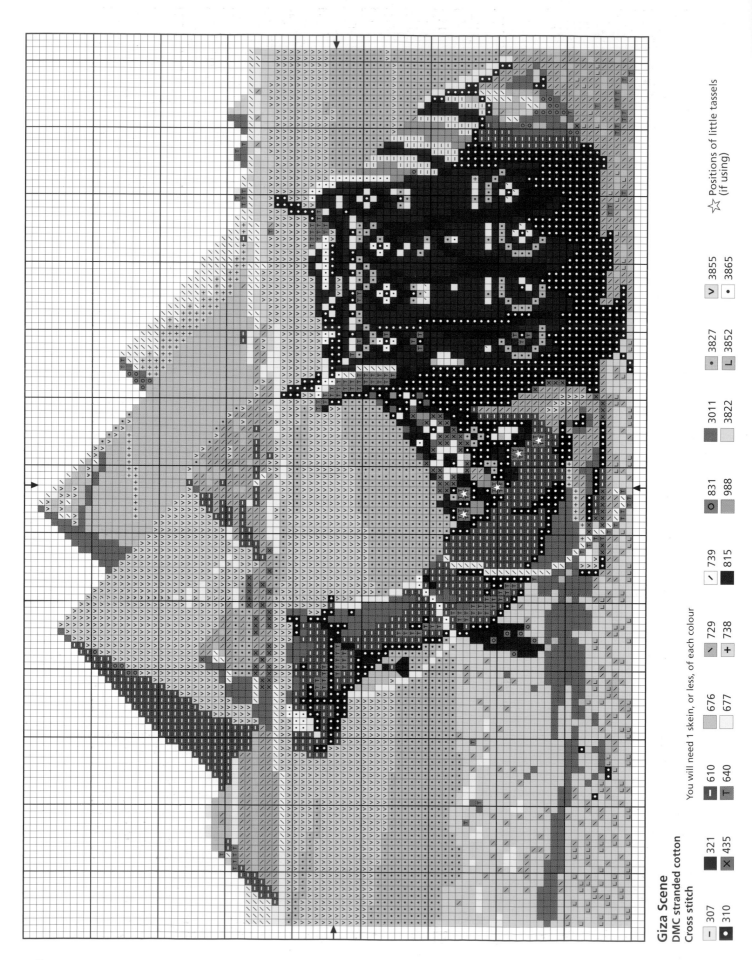

Giza Scene
DMC stranded cotton
Cross stitch

You will need 1 skein, or less, of each colour

-	307		610	/	676	/	729
●	310	T	640	+	677	+	738
■	321	O	831	/	739	L	988
X	435		3011	●	3827	V	3855
			3822		3852	●	3865

☆ Positions of little tassels (if using)

Ramesses Wall Hanging
DMC stranded cotton
Cross stitch

You will need 1 skein, or less, of each colour

Backstitch

● 433	✕ 435	I 437	T 640	╱ 739	╱ 890	�● 3371	3823	3855	— 844
434	436	520	– 738	844	○ 977	3782	╲ 3854	• B5200	— 3371

Decorative Hieroglyphs

Around 3,300BC the Egyptians invented a system of writing using picture signs called hieroglyphs, a Greek word meaning 'sacred carvings'. They are a highly distinctive and visual aspect of Ancient Egypt with a vast range of images, including people, animals, birds, insects and a multitude of inanimate objects.

Deciphering the hieroglyphics has brought the Ancient Egyptian world to fascinating life, revealing the actions of the pharaohs, the religious, political and cultural ceremonies and the details of everyday domestic life.

Hieroglyphics linked writing with painting and occurred in various forms – from hastily ink-written lists in domestic households to formal, ritual inscriptions elaborately carved, painted and inlaid on royal tombs and civic buildings.

A black-painted wooden coffin beautifully decorated with coloured hieroglyphs was the inspiration for a charming desk set of notebook, card, bookmark and trinket bowl. The symbols were chosen purely for their appearance not for their meaning. However, I included some I felt were appropriate – the writing set at the bottom right of the book cover is the sign for a scribe.

Ancient Egyptian hieroglyphs are simplified, stylized pictures and so make wonderful cross stitch designs, as this collection shows. The designs are very easy to stitch, worked just in full cross stitch with a small amount of backstitch. Stitching on dark fabrics like blue and black creates an instant sense of drama.

Trinket Bowl

Stitch count
32 x 30
Design size
5.8 x 5.8cm (2¼ x 2¼in)

Materials

🖎 7 x 7in (18 x 18cm)
14-count dark blue Aida
(DMC 796)

🖎 Tapestry needle size 24

🖎 Stranded cotton (floss)
as listed in chart key

🖎 10 x 10cm (4 x 4in)
fusible interfacing

🖎 Wooden bowl with lid
9cm (3½in) diameter
(see Suppliers)

1 Prepare your fabric and mark the centre lines with tacking (basting) – see page 99.

2 Following the chart on page 66, begin stitching from the centre of the chart and fabric, using two strands of stranded cotton (floss) for the cross stitch.

3 When the embroidery is complete remove the guide lines and press the work. Iron the interfacing on to the back of the embroidery following the manufacturer's instructions. Using the template provided with the bowl carefully cut the embroidery into a circle to fit into the lid, and then assemble according to the manufacturer's instructions.

Hieroglyphics offer a fascinating insight into everyday life in Ancient Egypt. Pintail ducks, for example, were a commonly seen bird. They occur in many paintings and are carved three-dimensionally into cosmetic palettes and jewellery. The bird often seems to be associated with fertility and sexuality. As a hieroglyph it occurs standing, where it stands for 'son or daughter of', and there are two forms of a flying duck.

Greetings Card

Stitch count
39 x 34
Design size
7 x 6.2cm (2¾ x 2½in)

Materials

- 🔱 10 x 15cm (4 x 6in)
  14-count dark blue Aida
  (DMC 796)
- 🔱 Tapestry needle size 24
- 🔱 Stranded cotton (floss)
  as listed in chart key
- 🔱 10 x 15cm (4 x 6in)
  fusible interfacing
- 🔱 Greetings card with
  8 x 8cm (3 x 3in) aperture
- 🔱 Double-sided adhesive tape

The owl is
an attractive
design, which was
frequently used.
Most hieroglyphic
signs had several
alternative
meanings: the owl
was often used
for its letter 'm'
meaning but could
also stand for the
word 'me'.

For centuries the hieroglyphic language was not understood, yet still intrigued people. They had heard that the Egyptians had millennia of knowledge and wisdom and assumed the hieroglyphs held the secrets, though in fact much of it lists names of rulers. Because the meanings had been forgotten, the language was seen as mysterious and secret, suitable for spells.

1 Prepare your fabric and mark the centre lines with tacking (basting) – see page 99.

2 Following the chart on page 66, begin stitching from the centre of the chart and fabric, using two strands of stranded cotton (floss) for cross stitch and one for backstitch.

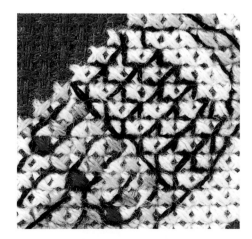

Most backstitches are the length of one Aida block but some diagonal lines reach from the corner of one block to the diagonal corner of the next block. Exceptions to this occur in the long lines defining the side of the wing towards the tip: take another stitch wherever the line crosses a hole between blocks and don't worry about two stitches that are quite long. Another unusual feature occurs with the beak, where the line moves from midway down a block to midway across a block.

3 When the embroidery is complete remove the guides and press. Iron the interfacing on to the back of the embroidery. Trim the fabric to fit your card and mount using double-sided adhesive tape (see page 101).

Bookmark

Stitch count
97 x 24
Design size
17.5 x 4.4cm (7 x 1¾in)

Materials

- 28 x 10cm (11 x 4¼in) 14-count dark blue Aida or 5cm (2in) Aida band in blue or with a blue edging
- Tapestry needle size 24
- Stranded cotton (floss) as listed in chart key
- 20 x 5cm (8 x 2in) iron-on transfer adhesive (such as Bondaweb)
- 20 x 5cm (8 x 2in) satin ribbon to neaten back

Understanding the hieroglyphic language remained a mystery until 1798 when a slab of granite was found near the town of Rashid, known to the Greeks as Rosetta. This slab, now called the Rosetta Stone, had three sets of texts – a top section in hieroglyphs, then a section of demotic script (a cursive derivative of hieroglyphs) and finally a passage in Greek but it took decades of study by various scholars to make connections between the three scripts.

A few hieroglyphs have survived the centuries in a recognizable form, such as this ankh sign for life and endurance, which is still used as a charm today. The motif also features on the notebook cover, opposite.

1 Prepare your fabric and mark the centre lines with tacking (basting) – see page 99.

2 Following the chart on page 66, begin stitching from the centre of the chart and fabric, using two strands of stranded cotton (floss) for cross stitch.

3 When the embroidery is complete remove the guide lines and press the work. Fold the long edges in and press and then fold over the short ends to make a bookmark 20cm (8in) long. If you have used Aida band you will only need to hem the short edges. Trim excess fabric to reduce bulk.

4 Bond the transfer adhesive to the ribbon backing by ironing and then peel off the backing paper. Place the bookmark face down on a thick layer of towelling on the ironing board and place the ribbon on the back of the bookmark. Press firmly to fuse the layers together.

Notebook Cover

Stitch count
160 x 114

Design size
29 x 20.5cm (11½ x 8⅛in)

Materials

- 36 x 78cm (14 x 31in) 14-count black Aida
- Tapestry needle size 24
- Stranded cotton (floss) as listed in chart key
- A4 notebook 29.5 x 21cm (11¾ x 8¼in)
- 30 x 46cm (12 x 18in) fusible interfacing (optional)

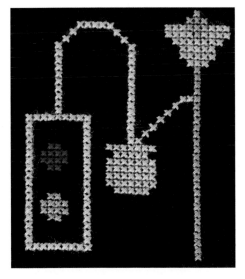

The scribe's set shows a palette that featured indentations to hold red and black pigment. This was attached to a rope which, at the other end, held a water pot and a container for brushes. The scribe carried it over his shoulder.

1 Prepare the fabric by folding the long side in half. With the fold on the left mark a line with tacking (basting) stitches 1.25cm (½in) from the fold to mark the left edge of the design. Find the centre of the shorter side and mark a horizontal guide line.

2 Following the chart on page 67, begin stitching from the left side, using two strands of stranded cotton (floss) for cross stitch and the grey backstitch, and one strand of black for the backstitch detail on the owl. Work the backstitch after you have completed the cross stitch – see step 2 of the greetings card on page 63 for details on working the backstitch on the owl.

3 When all the embroidery is complete remove guide lines and press the work. Making up into a book cover will depend on the size of your notebook – see page 102 for general instructions.

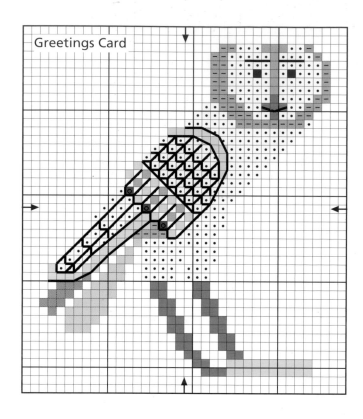

Greetings Card

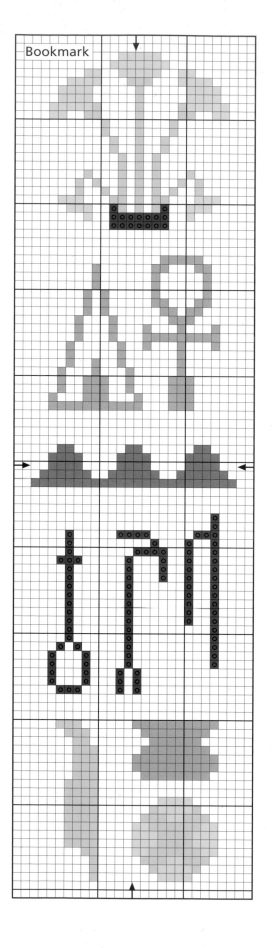

Bookmark

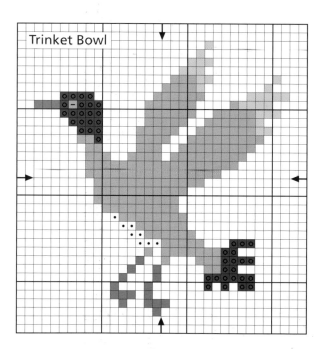

Trinket Bowl

Decorative Hieroglyphs
DMC stranded cotton

Cross stitch		Backstitch

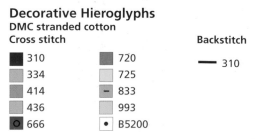

	Cross stitch			Backstitch
■	310		720	— 310
	334		725	
	414	–	833	
	436		993	
⊙	666	•	B5200	

Note: you will not need all of the colours for every design

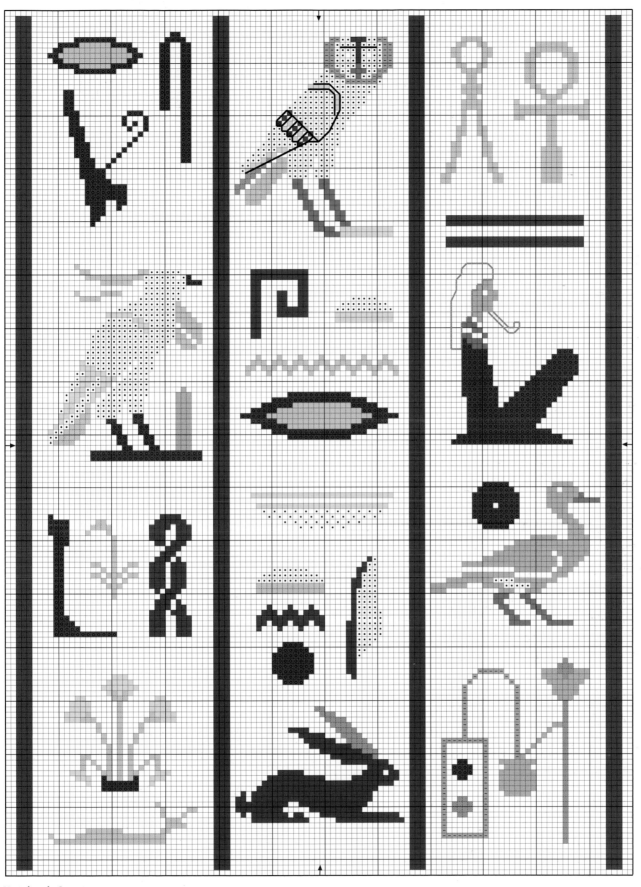

Notebook Cover
DMC stranded cotton
Cross stitch

					Backstitch
▦ 414	◉ 666	▨ 725	— 833	• B5200	— 310
▨ 436	▨ 720	▧ 797 (2 skeins)	▨ 993		— 414

Bastet, Cat Goddess

Bastet was a powerful and popular goddess. She was shown either as a cat or as a woman with a cat's head. Statues of her often include kittens because her maternal qualities were greatly respected. She shared attributes of fertility with other goddesses, such as Hathor and can also be identified with Sekhmet, the fierce lion goddess, though it was her more domestic, maternal and protective qualities, exemplified by her cat form, that became more popular.

By the time of the New Kingdom (1570–1070BC), cats had become tame and were prized domestic pets, valued for their company and mouse-catching abilities. Painted images from tombs show a cat sitting under the throne of a princess. Many small bronze statues of Bastet date from this period, and also hundreds of cat mummies that were dedicated to her at her temple. Every year a festival was held to celebrate Bastet and people made pilgrimages to her cult centre at Bubastis in the Nile delta to join the revelry.

Ancient Egyptian artists created many delightful animal studies, particularly cats, made from bronze and inlaid with gold and silver. The cat in my cross stitch design is based on a famous bronze statue adorned with gold earrings, which is held in the British Museum in London. The cat was sacred to the sun god and is often shown protecting the rising sun from the malevolent serpent. Khepri, the scarab beetle, a god of the sun and creation, and the solar eye are inlaid in silver on the cat statue's chest.

The papyrus background to my embroidery is based on the patterns shown in scenes of the banks of the Nile, some of which show cats climbing up the papyrus stems in search of birds. The papyrus plant, common in the delta area, symbolized freshness, flourishing growth, youth and joy and was a very useful plant, used to make an enormous range of items. Amulets were carried to bestow the papyrus qualities and Bastet is often shown carrying a sceptre in the shape of a papyrus.

This design uses many colours to suggest the form of the ancient statue and the patina of the bronze; this means there are places were many single stitches of various colours occur together. When finished it makes visual sense, but you will need to trust the chart. You will also need a good light and a degree of concentration. The backstitch detail of the eyes and paws is crucial but the chest motifs are optional.

Bastet Picture

Stitch count
138 x 90
Design size
25 x 16.3cm (9¾ x 6½in)

Materials

- 🗝 38 x 30cm (15 x 12in) 14-count oatmeal Zweigart Rustico Aida (code 54) or neutral 28-count evenweave
- 🗝 Tapestry needle size 24
- 🗝 Stranded cotton (floss) as listed in chart key
- 🗝 Suitable picture frame

In Ancient Egypt an annual festival was held at Bubastis to celebrate Bastet and according to the historian, Herodotus, it was an orgiastic experience. Vast quantities of wine were drunk and parties of pilgrims sailed up the river with flute players and women shaking sistrums (like castanets), dancing, shouting at the spectators on the banks and stripping off their clothes in an abandoned celebration of fertility.

1 Prepare your fabric and mark the centre lines with tacking (basting) – see page 99.

2 Following the chart opposite, begin stitching from the centre of the chart and fabric (working over two threads if using evenweave). Use two strands of stranded cotton (floss) for cross stitch and white backstitch and one strand for other backstitches.

3 When the embroidery is complete remove the guide lines and press the work. Frame as a picture (see page 101 for advice).

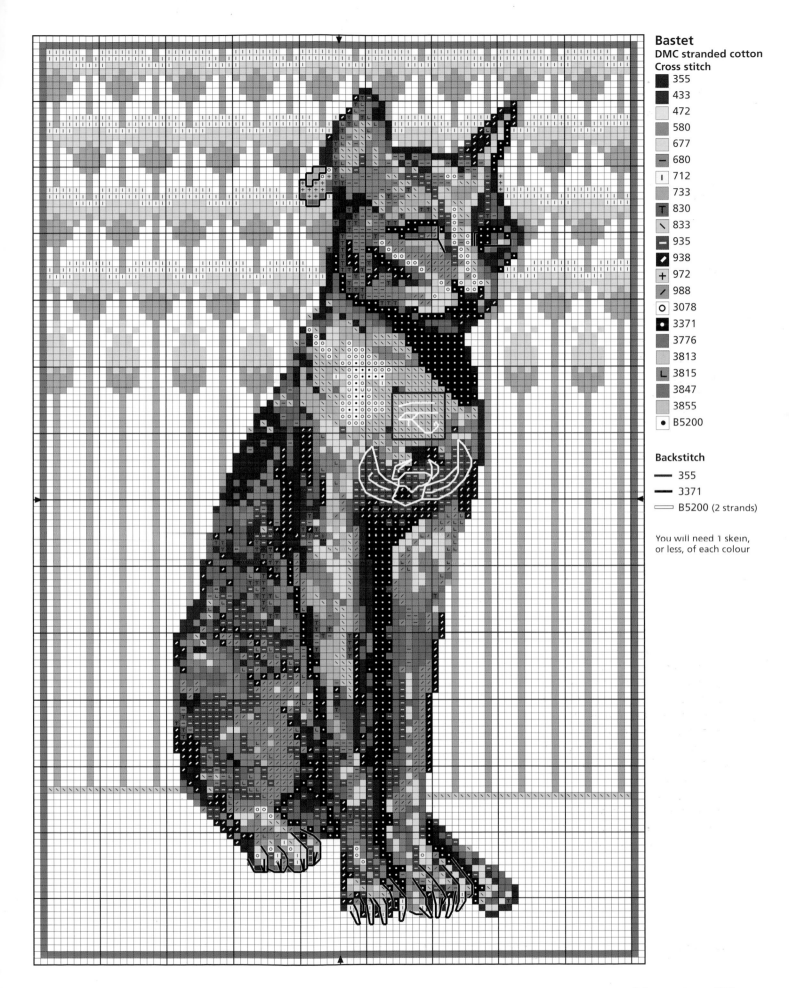

Bastet
DMC stranded cotton
Cross stitch

▣	355
▣	433
▨	472
▨	580
▨	677
−	680
I	712
▨	733
T	830
\	833
—	935
◪	938
+	972
∕	988
O	3078
◙	3371
▨	3776
▨	3813
L	3815
▨	3847
▨	3855
•	B5200

Backstitch

——	355
——	3371
══	B5200 (2 strands)

You will need 1 skein,
or less, of each colour

The Winged Scarab

You may think a scarab, or dung beetle, an unlikely choice to be credited with being the creator god, Khepri, who in Ancient Egyptian times rolled the sun across the sky every day. No doubt it was the beetle's habit of rolling a ball of dung in front of it that inspired this belief, and the observation that, miraculously, young beetles emerged from the dung balls, suggesting the power of spontaneous creation

These beetles also had an important role as protective amulets, placed over the heart of the deceased and inscribed with a text to prevent the heart from betraying any of its secret faults during the interrogation preceding the weighing of the heart ceremony. This ceremony was an important ritual in Ancient Egypt, forming a crucial part of the journey from death to the afterlife. The heart

of a deceased person was weighed in a scale against the feather of Ma'at, goddess of truth, harmony and justice. The heart and feather had to be in perfect balance because only then could the deceased be considered truthful and attain the status of blessedness in the domain of Osiris. Those found wanting faced annihilation by the 'Swallowing Monster', a hybrid of lion, crocodile and hippopotamus.

Scarabs were usually shown without wings, but the one I've used as the inspiration for this gloriously colourful and highly beaded evening bag is based on a very special jewelled scarab from the tomb of Tutankhamun. The wings give it a perfect shape for a bag and the colours are a real pleasure to work with. I've also designed an accompanying handbag mirror, which echoes the colours – see page 75.

This bag with its brilliantly coloured cross stitch and shining beads makes a striking accessory.
It is stitched on white fabric to make the beads glow even more but black would work well too.
The beads are sewn on using transparent beading thread, which is more durable than stranded cotton.

Scarab Bag

Stitch count
100 x 116
Design size
18 x 21cm (7⅛ x 8¼in)

Materials

- 30 x 30cm (12 x 12in) 14-count white Aida
- Tapestry needle size 24 and a beading needle
- Stranded cotton (floss) as listed in chart key
- Mill Hill seed beads as listed in chart key
- Transparent bead thread
- 0.25m (¼yd) of black satin for back of bag and lining
- 1m (1yd) black satin bias binding
- 20 x 50cm (8 x 20in) double-sided Rufflette Pelform for stiffening (or pelmet Vilene)
- 40cm (16in) cord for handle
- Magnetic fastening (from haberdashers)

1 Prepare your fabric and mark the centre lines with tacking (basting) – see page 99. Following the chart overleaf, begin stitching from the centre of the chart and fabric, using two strands of stranded cotton (floss) for cross stitch. If stitching on black fabric it will not be necessary to stitch the black area of the background, but you will need to make white stitches between the crystal beads on the sun disc (see below).

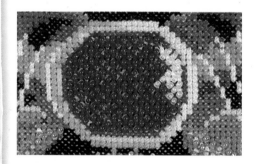

2 Stitch on the beads in the positions given on the chart, using a beading needle and transparent beading thread. When the embroidery is complete remove guide lines and press the work over a thick layer of towel.

3 Make up the bag as follows. Lay the bias binding face down on the right side of the embroidery. Pin and tack (baste) a smooth line around the edge of the design – it will pass through the cross stitches in places. Make sure that you achieve a symmetrical shape. Machine stitch the binding to the embroidery,

ensuring that the background fabric does not show between the embroidery and the binding. Join the ends of the binding neatly.

4 Turn over the embroidered piece and trim the excess fabric to the edge of the turning of the bias binding. Lay the trimmed piece on the Pelform and draw round the edge. Mark this as the front. Turn the embroidery over and draw round it again. Mark this as the back. Cut the pieces out and use them as templates to cut out a back to the bag and two pieces of lining.

5 Take the back fabric and repeat the binding as for the front. Now, on the right side, fold back the binding and press flat, just pressing the binding. Take the back stiffening and peel off the backing paper. Smooth the back fabric on to the stiffening. Repeat for the front. Attach the magnetic catch to the top of the two pieces of lining fabric, about 1.5cm (⅝in) from the top edge. Remove the paper from the insides of the stiffening pieces and attach the lining pieces to them.

6 Now hand stitch the bias binding to the lining fabric, front and back. Ladder stitch the front and back of the bag together invisibly, stitching the cord for the handle into the top of the bag as you go. Stitch beads to the cord to finish.

Mirror

Stitch count
41 x 41
Design size
6.5 x 6.5cm (2½ x 2½in)

Materials
- 15 x 15cm (8 x 8in) 16-count black Aida
- Tapestry needle size 24
- Stranded cotton as listed in chart key
- Iron-on interfacing
- Handbag mirror (see Suppliers)

1 Prepare your fabric and mark the centre lines with tacking.

2 Following the chart, begin stitching from the centre of the chart and fabric, using two strands of stranded cotton (floss) for the cross stitch and the backstitch.

3 When complete, remove guide lines and bond interfacing to the back (see page 101). Trim to fit the mirror and mount according to the manufacturer's instructions.

The mirror design was inspired by a head band featuring a gold chrysanthemum inlaid with red and green stones. The regularity of the flower was appealing to the Ancient Egyptians for this sort of diadem ornament. It was sometimes used three-dimensionally, with the petals curling around the base of a bowl. The shape can also be seen in the Royal Hunt wall hanging on page 30.

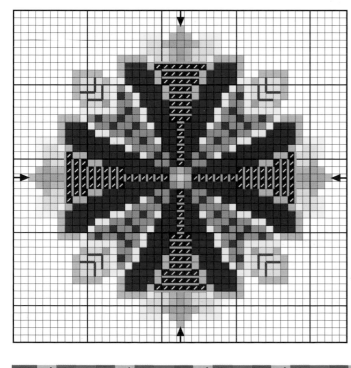

Mirror
DMC stranded cotton
Cross stitch

606	964
726	972
807	992
823	3809

Backstitch
- 807
- 3809

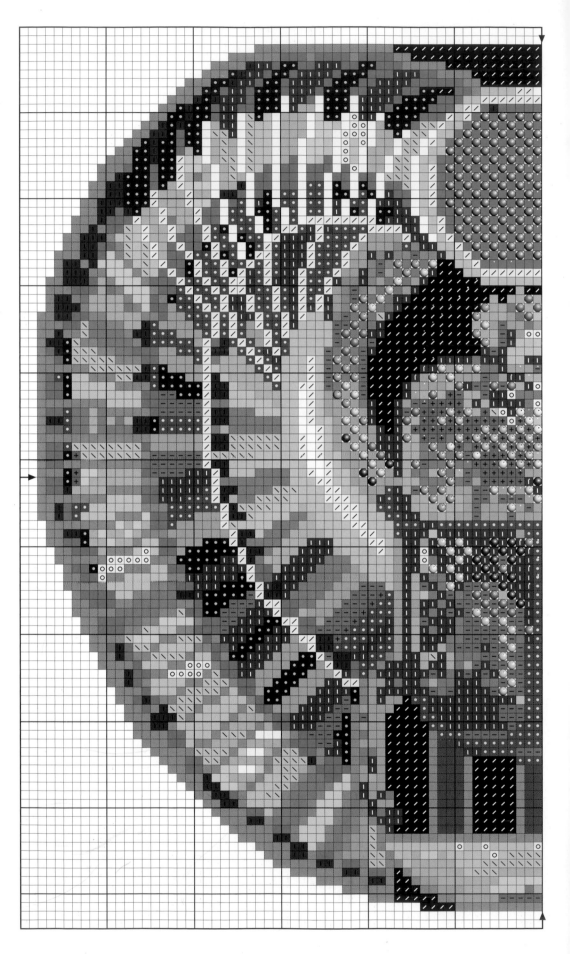

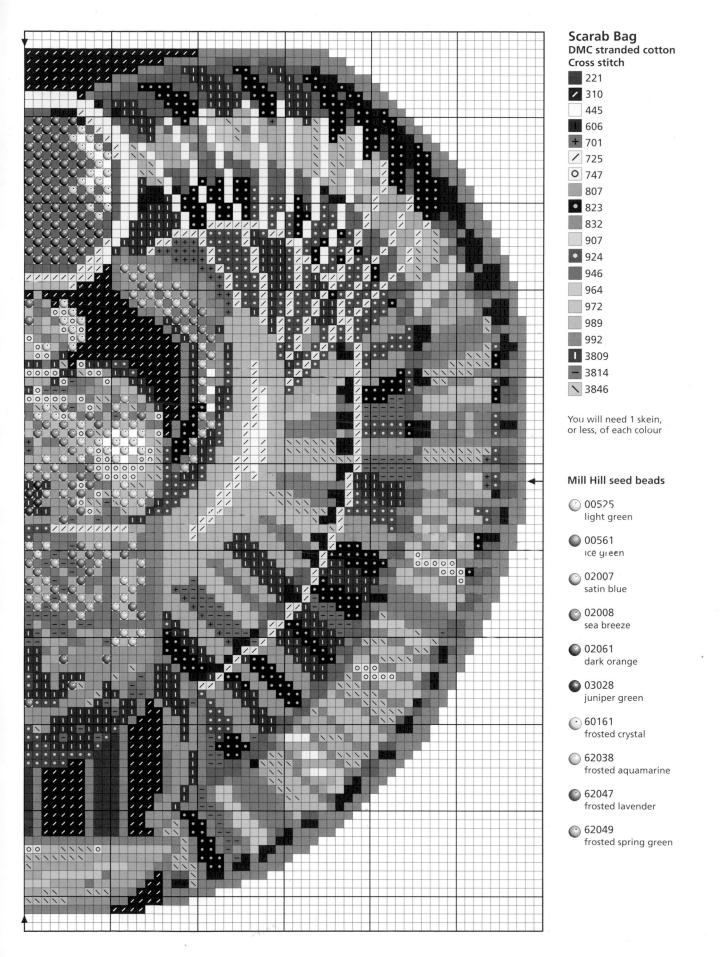

Scarab Bag
DMC stranded cotton
Cross stitch

- ◼ 221
- ⧄ 310
- ☐ 445
- ▮ 606
- ✚ 701
- ⧄ 725
- ○ 747
- ▨ 807
- ◙ 823
- ▨ 832
- ▨ 907
- ◍ 924
- ▨ 946
- ▨ 964
- ▨ 972
- ▨ 989
- ▨ 992
- ▮ 3809
- − 3814
- ⧅ 3846

You will need 1 skein,
or less, of each colour

Mill Hill seed beads

- ◉ 00525
  light green
- ● 00561
  ice green
- ◉ 02007
  satin blue
- ◉ 02008
  sea breeze
- ● 02061
  dark orange
- ● 03028
  juniper green
- ◉ 60161
  frosted crystal
- ◉ 62038
  frosted aquamarine
- ◉ 62047
  frosted lavender
- ◉ 62049
  frosted spring green

The Papyrus & the Lotus

The papyrus and the lotus were significant flowers in Ancient Egypt, one representing Lower Egypt and the other Upper Egypt. Papyrus used to grow thickly around the Nile and was extremely useful, used to build houses, to make rafts, mats, baskets, ropes and wickerwork, as well as paper.

The lotus was greatly admired in ancient times, both the white and the scented blue lotus. Legend has it that the blue lotus appeared from the primeval ocean on the first day of the world and the sun rose from it, so it symbolized rebirth and everlasting existence. It was used in bouquets as an offering to the gods and as a tribute to the dead.

I have used the papyrus and lotus flowers to create two elegant cushions. Both are bordered by patterns the Egyptians created from those flowers. The papyrus design was inspired by the decoration on an ancient mirror case. The lotus cushion is based on a jewelled pendant. Ideas for other projects using band patterns are given on page 81, followed by many charted bands on pages 90 and 91.

I have stitched the cushions on a sage green Aida fabric but you could use any other pastel shade instead. Only whole cross stitches are used and the colours, though there are some differences between the lotus and the papyrus, are designed to look well together.

Papyrus and Lotus Cushions

Stitch count
32 x 30
Design size
5.8 x 5.8cm (2¼ x 2¼in)

Materials (for each cushion)

- 46 x 46cm (18 x 18in) 14-count sage green Aida (Zweigart 611) or 28-count evenweave
- Tapestry needle size 24
- Stranded cotton (floss) as listed in chart key
- Backing fabric to tone with embroidery 46 x 46cm (18 x 18in)
- Cushion pad 38cm (15in) square

1 Prepare your fabric and mark the centre lines with tacking (basting) – see page 99.

2 Following the relevant chart on pages 82–89, begin stitching from the centre of the chart and fabric (working over two threads if using evenweave). Use two strands of stranded cotton (floss) for the cross stitch. When the embroidery is complete remove the guide lines and press the work.

3 Make up as a cushion cover as follows. On the embroidery, mark where you want the edge to be, bearing in mind the size of cushion pad you are using. Pin the embroidery and backing fabric right sides together and with the wrong side of the embroidered fabric uppermost, machine stitch around the edges following the marked line. Start a little way from one corner, go round three sides and finish by stitching a little way round the last corner, leaving a gap to put the cushion pad through. Work another line of stitching round the corners to reinforce them.

4 Cut diagonally across the corners, quite close to the stitching, and trim the other edges leaving a seam allowance of about 6mm (¼in). Turn the cover to the right side and press the seam. Insert the cushion pad and slipstitch the gap closed.

The word paper is derived from the word papyrus. Papyrus stems were split into narrow strips, which were laid side by side. Another layer of strips was laid on top at right angles and then the surface was sprinkled with water and beaten until the plant's juices ran out and bonded the pieces into a sheet. It made a durable writing surface, which could be glued to others and rolled around rods to form a scroll.

Band Designs

A selection of charted band designs, inspired by Ancient Egyptian decoration, has been provided on pages 90–91. These are very versatile and can be stitched to make up a wide selection of items, two of which are shown here. Choose your favourite bands to decorate bags or boxes or to frame samplers or photographs. The colours used in the bands can easily be changed, so why not experiment with creating your own colour combinations? If desired, the bands could also be used to replace the outer border on the lotus and papyrus cushions.

Borders are perfect for creating some quick-to-stitch bookmarks for family and friends, especially if you use Aida or linen bands with decorative edges.

Why not use one of the floral bands to embellish some bed linen? The shades can easily be changed to match the colour of your linen or bedroom.

Create a quick birthday gift by stitching a border as a simple patch to adorn a notebook or journal, sticking in place with double-sided tape.

A plain guest towel can be transformed into something quite special when decorated with a lovely band of lotus flowers. The colour of the towel was chosen to echo the colour of the flower buds. The design was worked on 5cm (2in) wide Aida band.

A drawstring toiletry bag decorated with a band pattern is very simple to make up. This lily design is based on the decorated handle of a dagger from the tomb of Tutankhamun and was worked on 5cm (2in) wide Aida band.

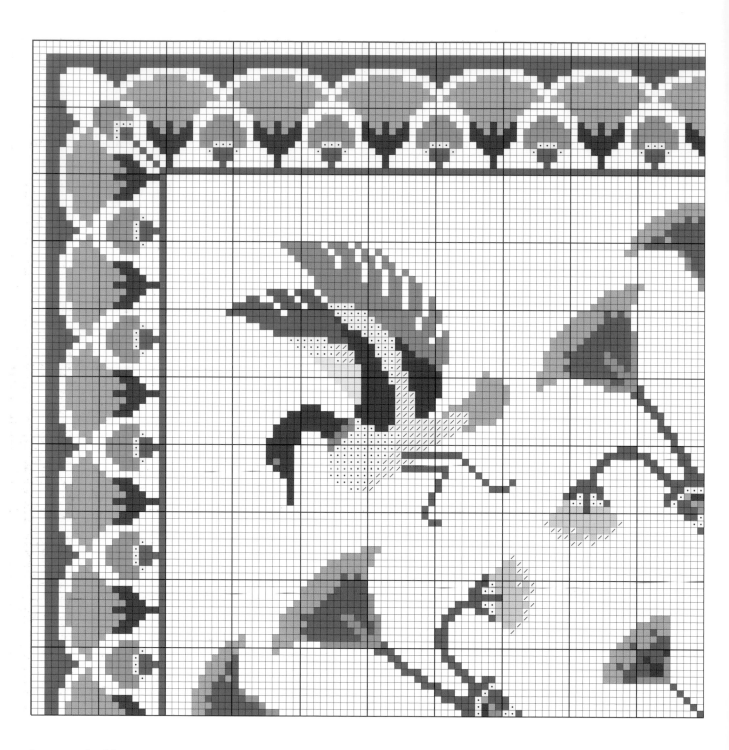

Papyrus Cushion
DMC stranded cotton
Cross stitch

■ 356 (2 skeins)	░ 747	▓ 922
▒ 598	■ 803 (4 skeins)	▓ 3847
╱ 746	▓ 826 (3 skeins)	• 3865 (4 skeins)

You will need 1 skein, or less, of each colour but 2 skeins each of 356, 3 skeins of 826 and 4 skeins of 803 and 3865

Papyrus Cushion
DMC stranded cotton
Cross stitch

■ 356 (2 skeins)	□ 747	■ 922
■ 598	■ 803 (4 skeins)	■ 3847
╱ 746	■ 826 (3 skeins)	• 3865 (4 skeins)

You will need 1 skein, or less, of each colour but 2 skeins each of 356, 3 skeins of 826 and 4 skeins of 803 and 3865

Lotus Cushion
DMC stranded cotton
Cross stitch

■ 356	▢ 747 (2 skeins)	▨ 922
I 597	■ 803 (5 skeins)	○ 996
▨ 598 (2 skeins)	▨ 826 (2 skeins)	• 3865 (4 skeins)

You will need 1 skein, or less, of each colour but 2 skeins each of 598, 747 and 826, 4 skeins of 3865 and 5 skeins of 803

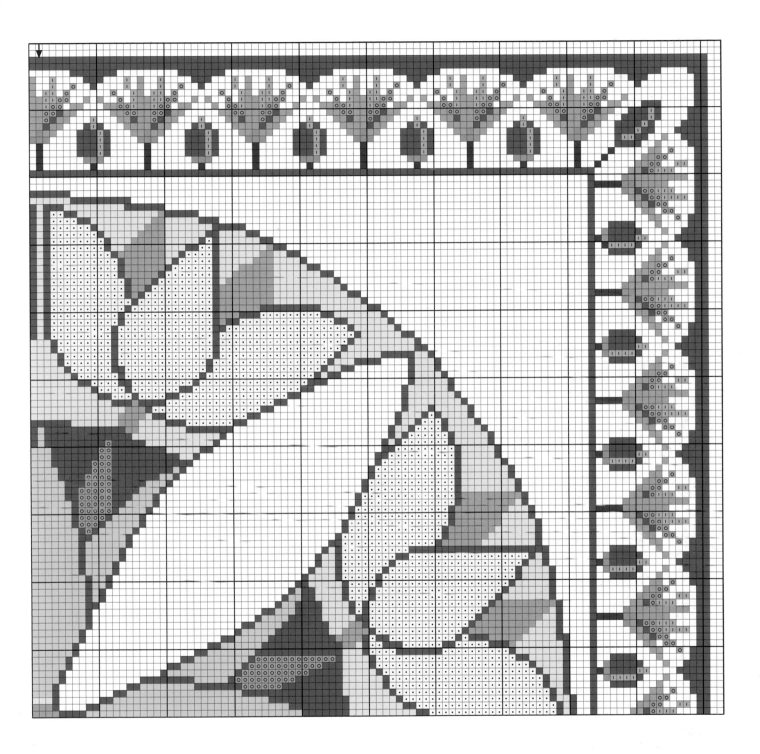

Lotus Cushion
DMC stranded cotton
Cross stitch

- ■ 356
- I 597
- ▨ 598 (2 skeins)
- ▨ 747 (2 skeins)
- ■ 803 (5 skeins)
- ▨ 826 (2 skeins)
- ▨ 922
- ○ 996
- • 3865 (4 skeins)

You will need 1 skein, or less, of each colour but 2 skeins each of 598, 747 and 826, 4 skeins of 3865 and 5 skeins of 803

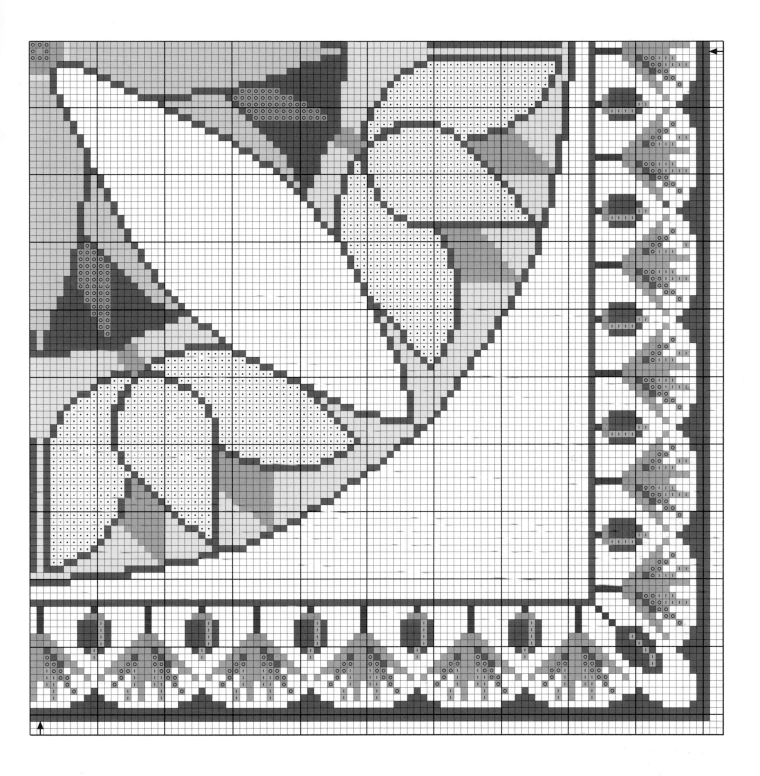

Band designs:
reds/blues
DMC stranded cotton
Cross stitch

598
726
820
900
972
3813
3816

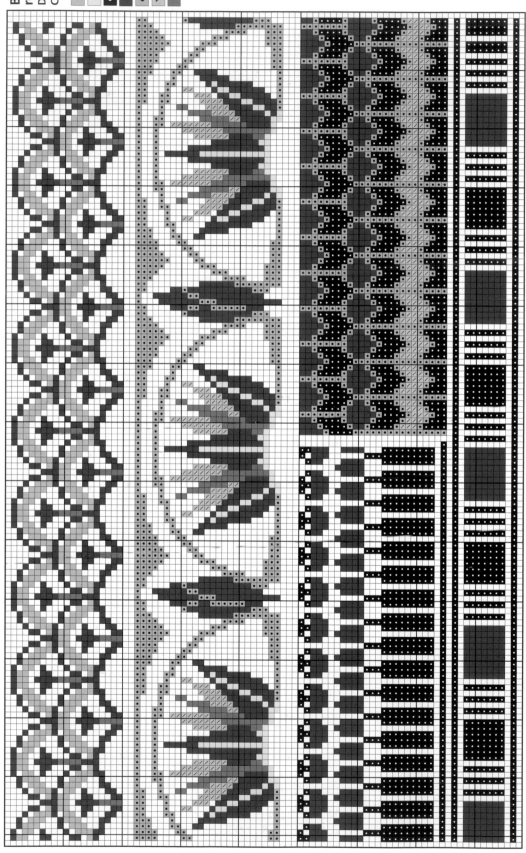

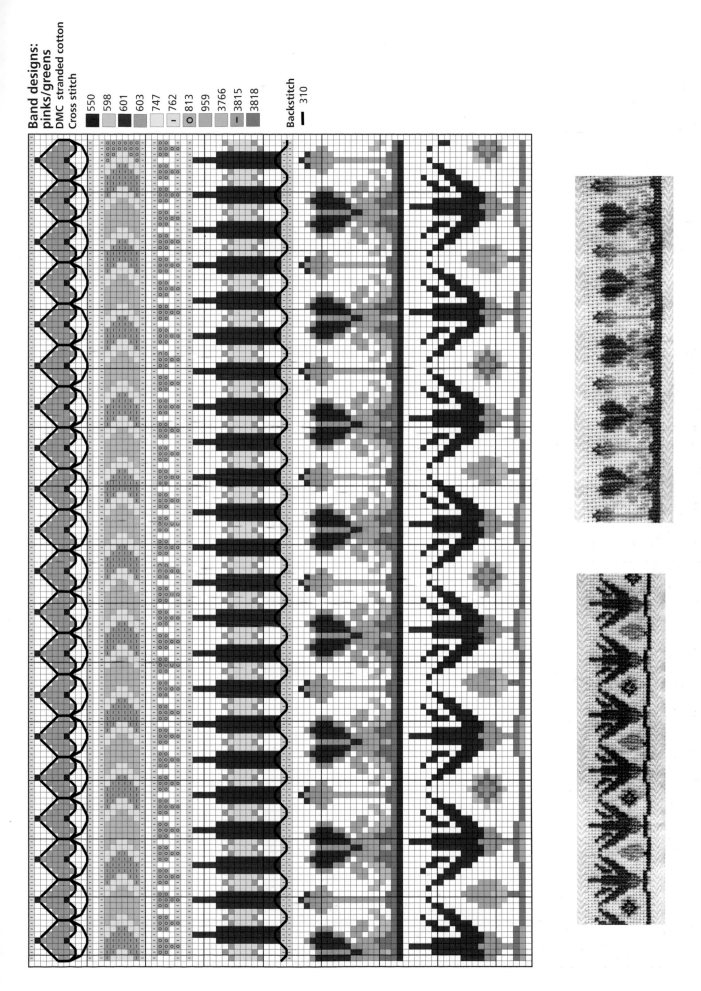

**Band designs:
pinks/greens**

DMC stranded cotton

Cross stitch

■	550
	598
■	601
	603
	747
−	762
O	813
	959
	3766
I	3815
	3818

Backstitch

| ▮ | 310 |

Life on the Nile

The Nile is the longest river in the world, rising in the East African highlands and flowing more than 6,500km (4,000 miles) to the Mediterranean. The rhythm of this great river was the most important feature in the lives of the Ancient Egyptians. Without the river Nile, Egypt would probably never have become a prosperous and powerful nation. It was an essential link between the low-lying delta area and the higher, drier territory of Upper Egypt, and goods were traded all along its length.

The Nile waters create a fertile band through the length of the country, able to sustain farming and produce enough food for a large population. Its regular yearly flooding was charted and valued as proof of the continuity of life, regularly reborn. The inundation between June and October every year deposited fresh, fertile silt allowing a wide range of crops to be grown, including wheat, barley, fava beans, lentils, peas, leeks, onions and many delicious fruits. Livestock and poultry were important too and were reared along the canals and villages that lined the Nile.

The river itself was an abundant source of food, home to many types of fish. Nile perch could even be caught in the irrigation ditches that were cut to channel water from the river to the fields. Early fishing boats were simple rafts made from bunches of papyrus reeds tied together and paddled with a primitive oar. These simple craft sufficed for crossing the river and fishing and continued for many centuries. For journeys up and down the Nile larger, sturdier boats were necessary. Wood had to be imported because Egypt had few trees. Masts and sails were added for the journeys down river but oars were still essential for travel in the other direction. The wooden boats had to be very shallow because the Nile had many mud banks.

These basic river craft were the inspiration for the two cross stitch embroideries opposite. In the top picture, a simple reed boat is being used by fishermen to catch fish using hooks and a net, while the other picture shows a more sophisticated wooden sailing boat – I adapted this boat from a tomb painting.

A yellow background was chosen for the two river scenes because this colour is often seen in paintings on tomb walls but you could also use a sky blue. These pieces rely on backstitch to convey details. The pictures were framed to allow a little extra 'sky' space above the action.

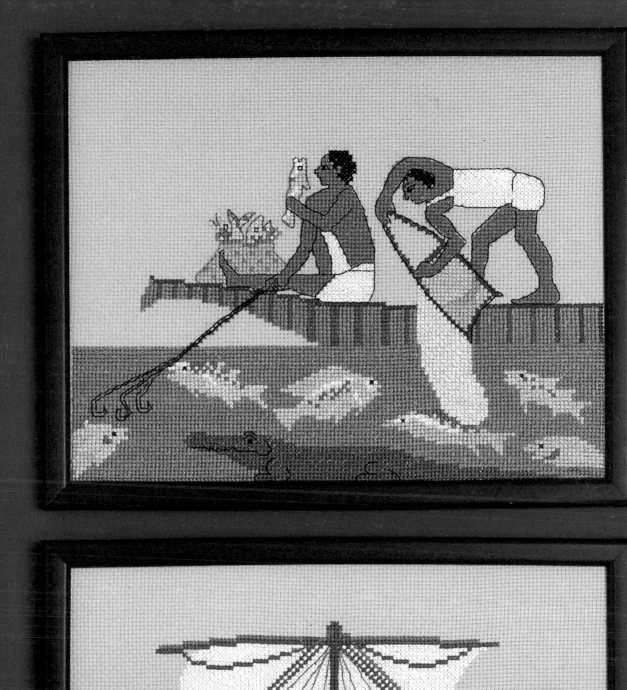

Fishing Boat Picture

Stitch count
85 x 135
Design size
15.5 x 24.5cm (6 x 9½in)

Materials

- 30 x 35cm (12 x 14in) 14-count yellow Aida (Zweigart code 2007) or 28-count evenweave
- Tapestry needle size 24
- Stranded cotton (floss) as listed in chart key
- Suitable picture frame

1 Prepare your fabric and mark the centre lines with tacking (basting) – see page 99.

2 Following the chart on page 96, begin stitching from the centre of the chart and fabric (working over two threads if using evenweave). Use two strands of stranded cotton (floss) for the cross stitch and then one strand for backstitch. Backstitch is vital to this design in order to represent the wonderful definition achieved by the painted relief of the original source. Wherever possible make a backstitch the length of one block of the Aida weave, though some stitches are longer and some of the shaping involves taking a new stitch halfway between chart lines.

3 When the embroidery is complete remove the guide lines and press the work. Frame as a picture (see page 101 for advice).

Boats were important for religious purposes as well as for simple travel. Re, the great Sun god travelled daily across the sky from east to west in a boat. Pictures of him survive in many paintings from the pyramids and tombs. Models show mummies being taken to the shrine of Osiris (Lord of the Afterlife) in Abydos. Egyptians enjoyed pilgrimages to shrines of popular gods, and all the important places were close to the river, which was Egypt's great highway.

Sailing Boat Picture

Stitch count
96 x 135
Design size
17.5 x 24.5cm (6¾ x 9½in)

Materials

🔆 30 x 35cm (12 x 14in)
14-count yellow Aida
(Zweigart code 2007) or
28-count evenweave

🔆 Tapestry needle size 24

🔆 Stranded cotton (floss)
as listed in chart key

🔆 Suitable picture frame

1 Prepare your fabric and mark the centre lines with tacking (basting) – see page 99.

2 Following the chart on page 97, begin stitching from the centre of the chart and fabric (working over two threads if using evenweave). Use two strands of stranded cotton (floss) for the cross stitch and then one strand for backstitch. Wherever possible make a backstitch the length of one block of the Aida weave, though some stitches are longer and some of the shaping involves taking a new stitch halfway between chart lines. There are some long stitches in the sail and the oars.

3 When the embroidery is complete remove the guide lines and press the work. Frame as a picture (see page 101 for advice).

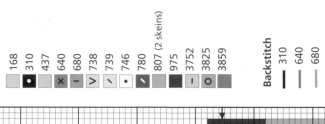

Fishing Boat
DMC stranded cotton
Cross stitch

▨	168
◉	310
▨	437
✕	640
−	680
∨	738
╲	739
•	746
◗	780
	807 (2 skeins)
▨	975
∣	3752
○	3825
◉	3859

Backsttich

▬▬▬	310
▬▬▬	640
▭▭▭	680

You will need 1 skein, or less, of each colour and 2 skeins of 807

If stitching the designs as a pair, 1 skein of many of the colours will suffice for both. You would need 2 skeins of 807, 2 of 746 and 2 of 780

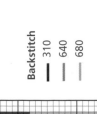

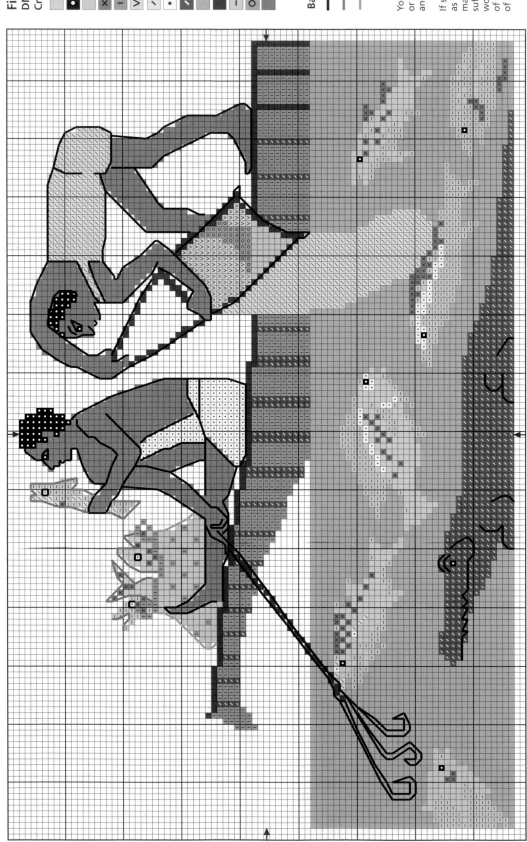

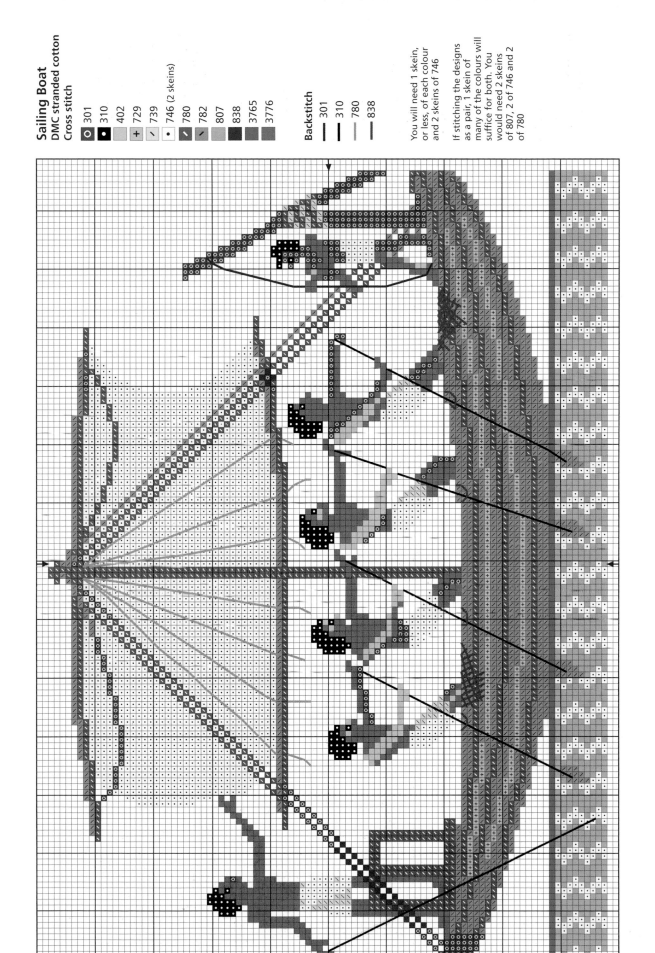

Sailing Boat
DMC stranded cotton
Cross stitch

◐	301
●	310
	402
+	729
╲	739
•	746 (2 skeins)
╱	780
╱	782
╱	807
	838
	3765
	3776

Backstitch

——	301
	310
	780
——	838

You will need 1 skein, or less, of each colour and 2 skeins of 746

If stitching the designs as a pair, 1 skein of many of the colours will suffice for both. You would need 2 skeins of 807, 2 of 746 and 2 of 780

Materials, Techniques and Stitches

This section describes the materials and equipment needed for the cross stitch embroideries
in the book, the techniques used and how to work the stitches.

Materials

Successful cross stitch embroidery requires only basic
materials and equipment readily available from good
needlecraft shops.

Fabrics

The projects in this book list the fabric required
for working the piece as in the photograph but you
can, of course, substitute one fabric for another. The
fabrics available may change as manufacturers launch
new colours or delete older ones – see the advice on
embroidery fabrics on page 103.

Aida is a blockweave fabric that is probably the
simplest to work. The weave locks each block of threads
in place resulting in a firm, very stable fabric.

Evenweave fabric, such as linen, has the same number
of warp and weft threads to 1in or 2.5cm. The gauge is the
holes per inch (h.p.i.) or the count. An evenweave is
usually embroidered over two threads at a time, while Aida
is stitched over one block. Thus a 28-count evenweave
fabric can be substituted for a 14-count Aida and a 32-
count evenweave for a 16-count
Aida, and vice versa.

If you wish to create a
more antique look to your
stitching, there are now Aidas
and evenweaves available
with special finishes to
mimic older fabrics. For
some projects I have used
'Vintage' fabrics, which are
overprinted with an antique
finish (as shown in the
picture, left).

Threads

The majority of the cross
stitch designs in this book
require only one skein
of each colour (or less).

Where a design needs more than one skein of a
particular colour, this information is given in the
chart key.

Stranded cotton (floss) Most of the projects use
stranded cottons; I used DMC but if you prefer Anchor
there are conversion tables available (ask at your local
needlecraft store) but bear in mind that colour matches
are not always exact. Always order colours by the
manufacturer's code number.

Ophir metallic thread This is made by Coats Craft and
is a three-ply thread twisted together into a single thread.
Use it as it comes.

Rayon floss This shiny thread is used just like a
stranded cotton.

Equipment

Needles Use blunt-ended tapestry needles for cross
stitch embroidery. I have recommended sizes, but you
may prefer a size larger or smaller: it is a compromise
between having an eye large enough to take the thread
and a needle that will pass through the fabric holes
without too much friction.

General accessories Apart from fabric, thread and
needles you must have a good pair of embroidery scissors
with sharp points, as well as fabric scissors. A bright light
is essential, preferably with a 'daylight' bulb. When you
work on dark fabrics it is helpful to place a sheet of paper
or white pillow slip over your knees to show the holes in
the Aida fabric more clearly. Working some designs will
be easier with a magnifier.

Frames I recommend using a frame for any evenweave
fabric and when working with a mixture of threads,
as their different characteristics may cause you to pull
some threads more than others. For small pieces a hoop
frame or flexi-hoop is suitable. Always try to use a frame
large enough to take the whole of the design. If this
is not possible then only leave the frame on the work
whilst you are actually embroidering, and take care when
repositioning it not to let the edge coincide with an
embroidered area. Visit your local needlework shop to
see a selection of frames.

Techniques

This section describes the techniques used for stitching the projects in the book, how to prepare fabric ready for stitching, how to use the charts and how to work the stitches.

Preparing the Fabric

When working on Aida I find that cutting it out with pinking shears is sufficient to stop it from fraying.

When using evenweave I like to neaten the edges by using a machine zigzag stitch or by overcasting the edges by hand.

The centre point on the chart is indicated by the use of opposing arrows. Find the centre of your fabric by folding it in half both ways. Mark the centre lines by tacking (basting) with sewing thread, making sure that the tacked line stays straight along the grain of the fabric. In some of the larger, more complex designs I have suggested marking extra guide lines – choose one colour for the centre guide lines and another for any other guide lines. I find a little time spent marking out greatly reduces counting mistakes.

Calculating the Design Size

As you gain confidence you may choose to work on a larger or smaller grade of fabric. This will of course result in the finished piece being a different size. To find out how large a piece would become divide the stitch count given by the number of holes per 1in (2.5cm) of the fabric (the count). Remember to then add at least 5cm (2in) extra on all sides to allow for making up – the fabric amounts listed in the projects allow for this. Where measurements are given the height is quoted first, followed by the width.

Following the Charts

Each coloured square on the charts represents one cross stitch. Backstitches and long stitches are shown by thick coloured lines and beads by larger coloured circles with a dot. As a general rule I start embroidering at the centre and work blocks of colour at a time.

The keys accompanying the charts have the threads used and their codes, plus an indication of where you might need more than one skein of a colour. Where necessary, symbols have been added to aid colour identification. The charts have slightly more pronounced lines every ten squares to help with counting.

You can use the charts straight from the book or photocopy them in colour for your own use. This allows you to enlarge and tape together sections of the larger charts. If you do this then you can cross off areas as you work them, which some people find helpful. It also allows you to draw in the centre lines and any extra guide lines in felt pen to match the guide lines you have worked on the fabric.

Starting and Finishing Stitching

Divide stranded cotton skeins into lengths of about 50cm (20in) and then divide each length into its six strands. Recombine the number needed for cross stitching – usually two.

To begin stitching in an empty area of fabric knot the thread then take it through the fabric from the front about 2.5cm (1in) from the starting point. When you have stitched over the thread the knot can be trimmed off and the end persuaded through to the back.

To start a new thread in a stitched area, just thread it under four or five stitches on the back of the work before beginning to stitch.

To finish off, thread your needle back through the last four or five stitches on the wrong side of the fabric and trim the thread.

Washing and Ironing Your Work

If you have to wash a piece of embroidery use a mild detergent well dissolved in hot water. Wash thoroughly without rubbing and rinse until the stain disappears. Never leave the embroidery wet. Remove excess water by rolling the item in a towel and squeezing gently. Dry it flat then iron from the back whilst still damp.

Careful pressing will smooth the fabric and correct any distortion without flattening the stitches and spoiling the texture. Lay the embroidery face down on a thick towel covered with a piece of sheet. Pull it into shape, making sure the fabric grain is straight. Press gently on the back at a heat suitable for the type of fabric and thread. Do not use steam on metallic threads (such as the gold used below) and cover the piece with a pressing cloth.

Stitches

There are very few stitches required to complete the projects in this book – cross stitch, of course, plus some backstitch and long stitch. Some projects have the addition of beads.

Backstitch

This is an easy outline stitch that is used in a few projects. The project instructions say whether it should be worked with one or two strands of cotton (floss). It is usually worked after the cross stitch over the same unit of fabric (one block or two threads) as you have used for the cross stitch. In this book backstitch is often required to contribute to fine definition and for this reason more irregular backstitches are used, sometimes moving one block to left or right but several blocks up or down. Wherever possible take a new stitch at the point where the line crosses an intersection on the chart. The project instructions give guidance.

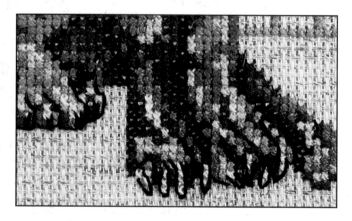

For a basic backstitch, follow the diagram below, first bringing the needle through the fabric from the back. Take a stitch from 1 to 2, bring the needle up again at the far end of the next stitch along the line at 3. Take another stitch backwards to fill in the gap.

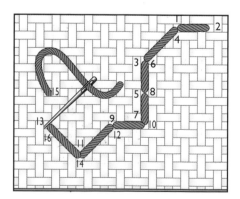

Cross Stitch

This is the basic stitch used throughout this book. Either work individual crosses, or work half crosses along a line, then return, stitching over the half crosses in the opposite direction. The first method is the most stable and unlikely to cause distortion and so is perhaps to be preferred if working without a frame. Either is suitable, as long as you develop an even tension without pulling the stitch so tightly that it distorts the threads of the fabric. Choose which direction your top stitch will go and stick to it. It is important to do this otherwise the texture will be uneven. Most of the designs in this book use whole cross stitches and no fractional stitches. The diagrams below show how to work cross stitch over one block of Aida or over two threads of evenweave.

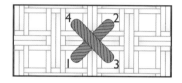

Cross stitch on Aida

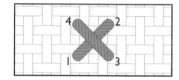

Cross stitch on evenweave

Adding Beads

Some of the designs use beads for extra sparkle and texture. Attach seed or bugle beads after the cross stitch and backstitch has been completed, using a beading needle or a very fine 'sharp' needle and thread that matches the fabric background or transparent thread if the bead is at all transparent.

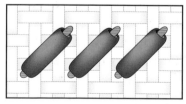

Attaching seed beads

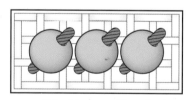

Attaching bugle beads

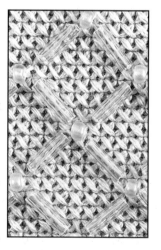

Making Up

This section describes how to make up the projects as they are shown in the book, but as the designs are very adaptable, you could make them up in many other ways.

Using Fusible Interfacing

Fusible (iron-on) interfacing is very useful for small projects where the fabric needs to be trimmed to fit and there is no room for turnings, for example, a bowl lid or paperweight. It is available in white and black for light or dark projects. Once ironed on it stabilizes the threads of the fabric, allowing an exact shape to be cut out without fraying. Always press the embroidery before adding the interfacing. Try a small sample on the fabric you are using first.

Mounting Work in Cards

There are many ready-made card mounts available today from various outlets. If desired, you can back the embroidery with fusible interfacing first (see above).

Check that your design fits the card aperture, trim the embroidery to slightly larger than the aperture and then attach it to the inside of the aperture with double-sided adhesive tape or craft glue. Press the card flap on to the back of the embroidery, using more tape or glue.

Stretching and Framing Work

To make your work up into a framed picture you can take it to a framer specializing in embroidery. If you prefer to do the mounting and framing yourself the following instructions should help. When framing behind a mount (mat) I sometimes just stick the embroidery to the backing card round the edges (though never allow glue on an area where it could be seen as a stain can develop over time). You could also try using the adhesive boards now available for embroidery.

Stretching If an embroidery is to be framed without a mount it will need to be stretched over a piece of stiff card (often called mount board). This method can also be used to cure wrinkles or distortions. Use white card for pale fabrics and dark card for darker designs.

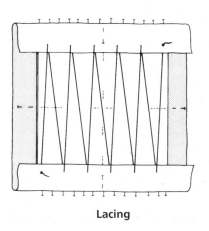

1 Cut the card to fit inside the picture frame, allowing for the thickness of fabric over the edges. Mark the centre of each side on the back of the card and mark where you want the centre of the embroidery to be. Lay the front of the card on the wrong side of the fabric, matching the centre marks.
2 Fold the fabric over the thick card and hold it in place by pushing pins into the card edges (see diagram below). Start at the centres and work outwards on opposite sides. Check that the fabric is held taut and that the grain is straight.
3 Take a long length of buttonhole or linen thread and lace from side to side, pulling the thread tightly enough to hold the fabric firmly in place without bending the card. Repeat this operation with the other two sides.

Lacing

Framing Many high-street shops now sell ready-made frames so there should be plenty of choice when choosing a frame for your work. I prefer to frame without glass, but if you do use glass make sure the embroidery isn't squashed up against the glass, flattening its texture. Use narrow strips of card at the edges of the frame, between the glass and the embroidery, to hold them apart. Clean both sides of the glass and then assemble the mounted embroidery in the frame.

Mitring a Corner This is a neat way of removing excess fabric from a corner and ideal for finishing napkins and similar items.

Fold the fabric in the required amount, mark the fold line and then unfold the turnings. At the corner, fold the fabric on the diagonal as shown in the diagram below and press the crease. Allowing for a small turning along the creased side, trim away the excess fabric. Turn in the long edges and the creased diagonal sides should meet in a neat mitre. Stitch them together invisibly.

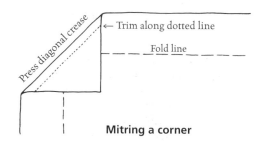

Mitring a corner

Making a Book Cover

These instructions are for the book cover on page 65 (shown below). Read through all the instructions first, so that you understand what the end result will be.

1 Measure from the opening edge of your book, round the spine to the other edge. Cut a piece of fusible interfacing this length x the height of the book (see diagram below) and bond it to the back of the fabric. Wrap the fabric round the front cover, the spine and the back cover. On the insides of the covers the fabric should come to within about 1.25cm (½in) of the spine. Check this measurement on your book to find the length of the strip and add a little ease at the top and bottom of the height of the book to allow for the thickness of the book's covers.

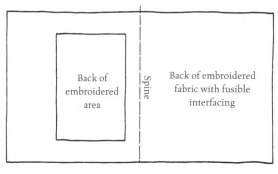

Making a book cover

2 Turn in the top and bottom edges of the fabric and neaten the ends. Wrap around the book to check the fit and then ladder stitch along at top and bottom to form the two pockets for the front and back covers (see diagram right).

3 Open the book and pull the covers back. Fold the embroidered cover inside out and slip the book covers into the pockets. It should be a close fit, but not so close that the book will not close completely.

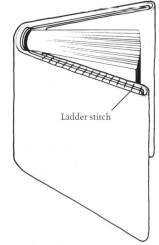

Wrapping the cover around the book

Suppliers

Coats Crafts UK
PO Box 22, Lingfield House, McMullen Road, Darlington, County Durham DL1 1YQ, UK
tel: 01325 394200 (consumer helpline)
www.coatscrafts.co.uk
For Anchor stranded cotton (floss) and embroidery supplies, Anchor Ophir metallic threads and Kreinik metallic threads

Coats and Clark
Greenville, SC 29612 0229 USA
tel: 800 243 08 10
fax: 864 877 61 17

Craft Creations Ltd
Ingersoll House, Delamare Road, Cheshunt, Hertfordshire, EN8 9HD
tel: 01992 781900
email: enquiries@craftcreations.com
www.craftcreations.com
For card blanks and accessories, including: owl card code AP10U in lavender 09 and papyrus card code DE10U in parch marque cream 10

DMC Creative World
Pullman Road, Wigston, Leicestershire LE18 2DY, UK
tel: 0116 281 1040
www.dmc/cw.com
For DMC fabrics, stranded cotton (floss) and other embroidery supplies

DMC Corporation
10 Port Kearny, South Kearny, NJ 07032-4612, USA
tel: 201 589 0606
www.dmc.com

Fabric Flair
www.fabricflair.com
For embroidery fabrics, including Zweigart

Framecraft Miniatures Ltd
Unit 3, Isis House, Lindon Road, Brownhills, West Midlands WS8 7BW, UK
tel/fax (UK): 01543 360842
tel (international): 44 1543 453154
www.framecraft.com
For Mill Hill beads and many pre-finished items with cross stitch inserts, including: wooden trinket bowl W3E and mirror HBM3

Heritage Stitchcraft
Redbrook Lane, Brereton, Rugeley, Staffordshire WS15 1QU, UK
tel: +44 (0) 1889 575256
email: enquiries@heritagestitchcraft.com
www.heritagestitchcraft.com
For Zweigart fabrics (including Juliana) and embroidery supplies

Kreinik Manufacturing Co Inc,
3106 Timanus Lane, Suite 101, Baltimore, MD 21244, USA
tel: 1 800 537 2166
www.kreinik.com
For metallic threads

Madeira Threads (UK) Ltd
PO Box 6, Thirsk, North Yorkshire YO7 3YX, UK
tel: 01845 524880
email: info@madeira.co.uk
www.madeira.co.uk
For Madeira stranded cotton (tel for thread conversion chart 01765 640003)

Madeira (USA) Ltd
PO Box 6068, 30 Bayside Court, Laconia, NH 03246, USA
tel: 603 5282944
fax: 603 528 4264

MCG Textiles Inc.
www.mcgtextiles.com
For embroidery fabrics

Mill Hill, a division of Wichelt Imports Inc.
N162 Hwy 35, Stoddard WI 54658, USA
tel: 608 788 4600
fax: 608 788 6040
email: millhill@millhill.com
www. millhill.com
For Mill Hill beads and a US source for Framecraft products

Riverbank Woodcrafts
tel: 07860 355820,
www.riverbank-woodcrafts.co.uk
For wooden boxes

Willow Fabrics (mail order)
95 Town Lane, Mobberley, Cheshire WA16 7HH, UK
tel: 0800 056/811
www.willowfabrics.com
For Zweigart embroidery fabrics

Embroidery Fabrics

Fabric manufacturers add new fabrics to their ranges and sometimes cease making older colours, so in case you have difficulty obtaining the fabric colours quoted in the project instructions, here are some alternatives you could try. (See above for details of manufacturers.)

Monument Panel – DMC have a similar type in their fabric range and so do MCG Textiles and Fabric Flair.
Tutankhamun and Egyptian Queen – Antique white is widely available from other manufacturers.

The Royal Hunt – An Aida is available or a neutral evenweave would also be suitable, or try DMC Marble Aida 3024.
Isis Picture – Not quite the same but fairly close to the smoky-violet used would be Aida code 3743 from DMC or a lilac from Fabric Flair code 519.
Falcon Box – Navy is also available as a DMC fabric code 792, and from MCG Textiles.
Magnificent Monuments – A similar sky blue is available from the DMC fabric range. The colour is available in cotton evenweave, Juliana code 5030 from Heritage Stitchcraft.

Decorative Hieroglyphics – A similar blue is available from Zweigart code 567.
Bastet Picture – A neutral coloured evenweave could be substituted for the oatmeal Rustico Aida.
Papyrus and Lotus Cushions – DMC have a similar colour (3053) or choose any pastel to suit your décor.
Fishing and Sailing Pictures – A sky blue could also be used.

Barbara's website www.wessexcollection.co.uk has a page on fabric substitutions and news about fabric availability.

Acknowledgments

For this, my fifth book of cross stitch designs, I have once again been grateful to all the friends who love cross stitch and who have stitched samples for this book. I thank them for generously offering their time and skill to help in the production of such lovely pieces.

I acknowledge help from the following stitchers: Ada Preston for the lotus cushion; Barbara Barnes for the Giza pyramids; Carole Smith for the Egyptian queen; Jennifer Bishop for so many pieces – the scarab bag, the hieroglyph notebook, Ramesses, Horus and Hathor and the papyrus card; Joan Harris has stitched many pieces as well – the falcon box, the Isis picture, the hieroglyph bookmark and owl card; Jo Bostock for Bastet the cat goddess; Kate Lydford for the sailing boat; Muriel Gray for Tutankhamun, the mirror and the border pattern for the toiletry bag; Rosie Minors for the Luxor temple; Stephanie Bramwell for the royal hunt and Valerie Ray for the papyrus cushion.

I also acknowledge the valuable help from my husband in calming me down when I have computer problems, working out what has gone wrong, and backing up my work regularly.

My editor, Cheryl Brown has made this volume possible and offered many valuable suggestions. I also thank Jennifer Proverbs, designers Prudence Rogers and Eleanor Stafford, and the photographers. My text editor and chart arranger Lin Clements has done a tremendous job.

Various companies have been generous in providing their products to use in the book. DMC have provided stranded cottons and fabrics from their range; Heritage Stitchcraft has supplied Zweigart fabrics; Framecraft Miniatures has provided a pot lid, handbag mirror, and Mill Hill beads and Riverbank Woodcrafts supplied a pad for the falcon box lid. Craft Creation supplied cards and Wendy Wools provided yarn samples. My thanks to all of them.

About the Author

Barbara Hammet is a designer who began her career teaching art and crafts and art history. Her interests then turned to embroidery, attracted by the colours and textures of fabrics and threads, and she now runs an established design business, Wessex Collection Embroidery, specializing in historic designs. She has had four books published by David & Charles, as listed below. Barbara lives in Winchester, Hampshire, UK.

Other books by Barbara Hammet, published by David & Charles:

- THE ART OF WILLIAM MORRIS IN CROSS STITCH
- ART NOUVEAU CROSS STITCH
- CELTIC ART IN CROSS STITCH
- ELIZABETHAN CROSS STITCH

Index

Pages in **bold** indicate charts